CATCH UP WITH TOP ACHIEVERS
2019 HSC EDITION

By Adam Ma and Fionn Parker

Copyright © 2019 by Adam Ma

The moral rights of the author have been asserted

All rights reserved.

Except as permitted under the Australian Copyright Act 1968 (for example, a fair dealing for the purposes of study, research, criticism or review), no part of this book may be reproduced or used in any manner without written permission of the copyright owner except for the use of quotations in a book review.

For more information, email: cuw.top.achievers@gmail.com

 A catalogue record for this book is available from the National Library of Australia

First paperback edition May 2019

Book design by Grzegorz Japoł (www.book-cover.design)

Editing by Huaiyu Wang/ Fionn Parker

Cover image: iStock

ISBN 978-0-6485633-0-3 (paperback)

ISBN 978-0-6485633-2-7 (EPUB)

ISBN 978-0-6485633-1-0 (Kindle)

Disclaimer
The material in this publication is of the nature of general comment only, and does not represent professional advice. It is not intended to provide specific guidance for particular circumstances and it should not be relied on as the basis for any decision to take action or not take action on any matter which it covers. Readers should obtain professional advice where appropriate, before making any such decision. To the maximum extent permitted by law, the author and publisher disclaim all responsibility and liability to any person, arising directly or indirectly from any person taking or not taking action based on the information in this publication.

TO CRANBROOK SCHOOL,
THE HIGH SCHOOL
AFFILIATED TO RENMIN UNIVERSITY OF CHINA,
AND
BEIJING WANQUAN PRIMARY SCHOOL.

YEET.

CONTENTS

Introduction	9
About the authors	12
How to use this book	15
Growth through doing	17
The key to successful Biological study *Alexandra Christopoulos*	19
Business studies and General tips from First in the State *Tim Yang*	33
Physics: Is there are dream too big? *Jesse Wright*	41
Modern History *Zoe Zhang*	51
Becoming a Drama Queen *Drew Ireland-Shead*	65
Success with Economics *John Bivell*	95
Be a Top-Achiever in Geography and Chemistry *Eleanor Lawton-Wade*	105
How to put the Study in Legal Studies *Jenny Wang*	127
Surviving and Conquering HSC General Mathematics *Lucinda Krek*	139
How to Ace Music 1 *Varun Mahadevan*	149
Major Keys to Music Success *Belinda Thomas*	157
PDHPE and Earth and Environmental Science *Lucy Stevenson*	169
Afterword	185
Acknowledgement	187

Introduction

"You don't need to start taking things seriously until you are in Year 12."

There are a lot of myths about your final year of study. Indeed, phrases such as "rank doesn't matter," or "I'll just lift for externals," are commonplace around the common room. These misconceptions are black holes for HSC students, becoming quagmires of procrastination and, ultimately, disappointment.

However, of all these myths, there is none more damaging, none more infamous, than the classic "nothing counts until year 12."

You may have been a Year 7 student when you first heard this. You were probably freaking out about your French vocab test, cramming the answers in at lunch time with your best mate. Oblivious to your anxiety, a burly Year 12 student with a flimsy beard (which you falsely take as a sign of maturity) practically trips over you as he saunters through the corridor.

"What are you doing?" he booms.

"Just studying for my t-t-test n-next period," you manage to splutter, shocked he has even recognised your existence.

"Studying? Mate, let me give you some advice - nothing counts until Year 12." As he strides away, his chortling laugh washes over you, shaming you for your studiousness.

The thing is, that kid couldn't have been more wrong. In all honesty, he was probably employing the same study-technique cocktail of procrastination and mass memorisation as that Year 7 kid. There is one difference: he is doing it in Year 12, when the stakes are much higher!

What he fails to recognise, to his detriment, is that whilst marks from previous years do not directly influence your ATAR, the effect that they have on how you prepare and ultimately perform in the final exams cannot be overstated.

The earlier years (in particular Years 10 and 11) are where you build the bedrock of writing, learning and critical thinking skills. These will serve you in good stead for the HSC year and beyond.

You cannot expect to simply go from an 11/20 to a 20/20 over the course of a few months, simply because you are going to "actually start trying now," (the amount of times I heard this line throughout Year 12 was pretty shocking)!

The fact is that the exams that you are subject to in the earlier years often mirror the nature of the HSC quite closely. This is the time where you hone your memorisation skills, develop your essay writing structure, and practice your exam techniques. You can figure out what works and what doesn't, as well as how much effort is required to perform to the best of your ability.

Just as doing HSC past papers will help you prepare for the final exams, the effort that you put in during the earlier years will give you a platform to keep your results at a consistently high level, as well as alleviate many of the significant stresses of the Year 12 workload, by having confidence in your previously established skills. It gives you time to work on developing that 'X-factor', the 'personal voice' and the 'point of difference' that teachers love, rather than just haphazardly trying to nail down the basics.

"Hard work beats talent when talent doesn't work hard," my Year 9 Mathematics teacher, Ms. Cooper, used to say. What she meant is that you can't expect to fly by on your own natural intelligence through the earlier years, even if you are getting adequate results. This is because when you get thrown into the deep end of year 12, the fact of the matter is, you won't know how to swim.

To probably erroneously use another's words once more, "I fear not the man who has practiced ten thousand separate kicks at once," said Bruce Lee, "but the man who has practiced one kick ten thousand times." By giving yourself a base of skills, by knowing how to succeed and what success feels like through your early years, preliminary exams and internals, you may just break the wooden board that is the HSC!

What can students do to reach their maximum academics potentials?

The idea of creating a book came to us. We noticed that schools often neglect the teaching of study skills.

In this book, you will learn about how past HSC Top-Achievers approached their academics throughout high school. Each of them has conquered high school by achieving great HSC results. One ancient Chinese proverb goes: "you can lead a horse to water, but you can't make it drink." It is your responsibility to have clarity when you go into your senior years in high school. We will do our best to help you, to set you onto the right path to a successful journey.

Adam Ma

Adam is the editor-in-chief *Catch Up With Top-Achievers: 2019 HSC Edition*. He graduated from Cranbrook School, Sydney in 2018 with an ATAR of 98.4. He is currently completing a bachelor's degree in Computer Science at University of New South Wales.

He is also the founder and director of Tree Niu Bee Pty. Ltd, a Start-up company that focuses on technology and education.

Catch Up With Top-Achievers: 2019 HSC Edition is his debut work in the book publishing industry. He wishes to enlighten younger students to become life-long learners.

Fionn Parker

Fionn Parker, finished Year 12 in 2018, graduating from Cranbrook School as Dux and with an ATAR of 99.95. As a writer, Fionn won multiple prizes throughout his scholastic career for both poetry and prose, whilst also being a long-term student writer for the school paper. He runs a successful Cricketing Social Media Page on Facebook known as 'Smart and Engaging Australian Cricket Memes,' and is currently working as a private tutor. He is currently studying a double degree of PPE/LAWS at ANU as a recipient of the National University Scholarship.

About the Top-Achievers

The contributors of *Catch Up With Top-Achievers: 2019 HSC Edition* have all achieved exceptional results in the 2018 HSC. All of whom have achieved one or more State-Ranks in their HSC subjects. They took out their valuable time to share their wisdoms with the hope to enlighten the readers.

1. Alexandra Christopoulos – 9th in Biology
2. Tim Yang – 1st in Business studies
3. Jesse Wright – 7th in Physics
4. Zoe Zhang – 1st in Modern History
5. Drew Ireland-Shead – 2nd in Drama
6. John Bivell – 1st in Economics
7. Eleanor Lawton-Wade – 3rd in Geography, and 7th in Chemistry
8. Jenny Wang – 4th in Legal studies
9. Lucinda Krek – 1st in General Mathematics 2, and 3rd in PDHPE
10. Varun Mahadevan – 2nd in Music 1
11. Belinda Thomas – 3rd in Music 2
12. Lucy Stevenson – 1st in PDHPE, and 2nd in Earth, and Environmental Science

How to use this book

Unfortunately, simply reading this book will not make your grades go any higher. However, this book might spark new ideas and values that you have never thought about previously. For this reason, you can consider this book as a starting point of your journey to take charge of your academic life.

If you are already on the right path to becoming a Top-Achiever, well done for wanting more! We guarantee that you will find something useful in this book that can assist you to achieve even better results.

There is lots of useful advice in this book, and you might be overwhelmed at first. Therefore, we recommend you follow the listed steps below to begin your reading:

1. Get a highlighter or a pen.
2. Skim through the book, focus on the **headings** and highlight what you would like to know more about.
3. Read through thoroughly the sections that interest you.
4. Implement these tips into your studies
5. Repeat the process.

As you become more familiar with your study habits, you will discover your own ways of using this book.

Be persistent. If something doesn't work out at first, try again. However, remember that you need to be flexible with your goals and approaches; don't be afraid to ask for assistance if you are stuck.

Grow through doing

"The man who asks a question is a fool for a minute, but the man who does not ask is a fool for life"- Confucius.

You explore your passions through many years of schooling. Some students find their passion from early on while others find theirs later.

We are all different. In the course of going through high school, you will encounter subjects that you find interesting, while others are boring. Despite many criticisms with the current system, most of us have the resources to learn about what we are passionate about. From learning to start a business, or to composing sheet music, high school is no doubt an important period for personal growth.

When you begin to doubt your education (which is completely normal), think back to the original question: "What is the purpose of learning?" The greater understanding you have about YOUR purpose of learning, the higher the chances you will succeed in the classroom! The same applies for everything, because without a clear purpose, you will have a hard time to reach your goals.

It is okay to doubt from time to time. It means you are thinking independently. However, as cliché as it sounds, there is a reason behind everything. For example, when I was learning sketch curves on a Cartesian plane, I had a hard time understanding its purpose. As the difficulty increased, I also discovered that sketching curves could also be used to finding solutions to simultaneous equations, or examine the behaviour as the values of variables approach specific values.

You may not understand the purpose of one thing immediately, but that is the most beautiful piece of the puzzle you'll need to solve. What is the purpose? Is the purpose to develop a sequential thinking skill? Or is the purpose to learn from the past so that we can prevent similar events to happen in the future?

Instead of grumbling about your lack of learning at school, you need to take charge of finding your ultimate path. You grow through doing. If something does not work out, learn from your mistakes and try something else. High school is the best time to experiment with new activities and to understanding your true self.

In the following chapters, top-achievers will explain how they worked towards becoming the best version of themselves during the HSC year.

THE KEY TO SUCCESSFUL BIOLOGICAL STUDY

An outline of my successes and experiences with the 2018 Biology HSC

By Alexandra Christopoulos

> *"We are here to laugh at the odds and live our lives so well that death will tremble to take us."* – Charles Bukowski

Introduction

My name is Alexandra Christopoulos and I am a 2018 Graduate of the HSC. Since the age of five until graduating year I had attended a school in the city known as Ascham School. High school for me was an unforgettable experience filled with countless adventures and friendships I'll carry with me for the rest of my life, but it was simultaneously one of the most stressful times of my life. Through my experiences with high school I have come to the belief that there is too much anxiety and pressure surrounding students sitting their HSC. When this is coupled with hardly any direction or advice on how to study effectively it can inevitably lead to many students, like myself at the time, feeling hopeless and overwhelmed when it comes to studying for their end of school examinations. That being said, I was lucky enough to have parents who sacrificed nearly everything for me to be able to attend a good school, which provided me with the opportunities to seek out the right people for advice on what study methods were the most effective when endeavouring to prepare for my biology examinations. My hope here is to convey which study methods I found were best for studying biology, and what I consider to be the most effective way to manage and plan your time when it comes to sitting the HSC. My goal is to provide all struggling students with the right foundational skills for biology study, so that they can have an equal opportunity to gain the most that they possibly can from the HSC and all future studies.

Since I was a little girl my ambition has been to help people, to protect and support others especially when they are feeling the most vulnerable. For this reason, I have always been passionate about pursuing Law and most especially bioethics, so that I can combine my love for biology and the pure sciences with assisting those in need. Upon discovering that the ATAR requirements for such a degree were increasingly high, I realised that there was an urgent need to fine tune my studying and preparation skills in order to gain the very most from my HSC. I know many others will be confronted with the same challenges I have faced, so these next few pages will act as a guide to shape how you approach your study and work ethic.

1. Surviving the HSC

Initially when I was confronted with the looming prospect of HSC, I was overwhelmed, extremely overwhelmed! All those countless exams, rankings, averages, scaling, and moderation. At times it seemed ridiculously complex, and biology in relation to this was no different. However, the major misconception about HSC biology was that it's all about memorisation. This should not be accepted as the truth, as simple memorisation will provide you with around band 4 levels results.

In order to achieve those band 6 results, more focus should be placed into approaching stimulus based questions and the technique to do so, rather than just simply learning content. Another misconception about HSC Biology was that it should be avoided because "it doesn't scale well." This I can comfortably say is a completely false notion. From my experiences and from those of my peers, scaling should not be a determinant in choosing subjects; choices should be based on passion and ability. Scaling will not downgrade any results if you are proficient in the subject. That is my primary rule to consider when 'surviving the HSC.' This same rule applies for subjects that apparently scale well. In these subjects you will not automatically do well because of the scaling. You still need proficiency in the subject for scaling to work for you, or otherwise it will send you backwards. The second rule I have is study smart, not hard. I know this is a completely overused phrase, but it could not be more true when approaching months upon months of consistent study. Study and revision should not be torture, and yet again, contrary to popular belief it should not necessarily consist of pages upon pages of notes scrawled down. Study rather should be catered to the type of learner you are: whether you are tactile, auditory or visual. Yes, studying will inevitably involve some writing and note taking, but should not be exclusive to it. But I will explore this in more detail further on. Finally, one of the most important tips I have on surviving the HSC is to do with stress and motivation. The period between trials and the HSC for me was one of the toughest times to find motivation. After putting all my effort into study for trials doing it all again seemed simply unimaginable. This is where finding motivation is important. When it comes to sustaining motivation, the most important method in doing so is ensuring a healthy balance between exercise, health, friends and family and study. In my experience this helped maintain perspective and avoid feelings of helplessness and exhaustion that come from constant study. The same applies to stress management. Stress was particularly an issue for me and I found the most effective way to deal with it was to maintain perspective, whether that was through talking to older friends or family about their experiences with the HSC, or taking a walk on my local beach to clear my head. When it comes to your own methods for stress relief and building motivation, it's important first to ask those closest to you for advice and find ways that are best for you to clear your head when it gets overwhelming, taking breaks when needed. It doesn't matter if those breaks are as short as a few minutes to chat with a friend or grab a snack, as long as they allow you to step away from study for at least a moment or two.

2. HSC Biology

As stated, HSC Biology is a subject that has many presumptions surrounding it, whether it is in regards to difficulty, scaling or study techniques. What I plan to achieve in this section is to question some of these assumptions, and explain how I would approach Biology as a subject in terms of confronting difficult topics and attitudes towards learning. I would also like to provide some last-minute tips from my experiences in the classroom while being taught the biology content. When it comes to confronting difficult topics, most people become overwhelmed and afraid of the topic and try to limit their exposure to the content. Whether it's through avoiding study regarding the topic, or simply ignoring homework, or study questions or task. This is counterintuitive and will send you backwards in terms of navigating biology. To combat this fear, I can place no stronger emphasis on asking questions, not just in the classroom but outside of the classroom. When I was overwhelmed in biology, the content regarding *meiosis* was a frequent offender, and initially like everyone else I freaked out. But after realising that this would get me nowhere, I begin to ask myself, "what don't I understand?" Then I would write various points down and research as much as I could about them, not just on the HSC websites, but also all over articles and journals, even rudimentary kid's websites if I was really stuck! The truth is, when starting to learn something that you know you'll struggle with, the best thing to do it to break it down into smaller bite size chunks, and deal with these individually, so that the content seems less intimidating. If this fails, bring these questions to a teacher and ask them if you would be able to work through the questions you have together. This is where the importance of asking questions becomes so crucial. Through asking yourself about what you don't know and writing things down, you have essentially provided yourself with a map to the holes in your knowledge. This in turn can be brought to a teacher, or a peer who is proficient in the subject, showing them clearly how they can help you. This approach of questioning enables you to unlock information that you would not otherwise access, or not think to consider. In my experience this technique of self-questioning is invaluable to learning biology content, answering test questions, and succeeding overall in the subject. Finally, when it comes to general advice in achieving great results in Biology, I would say there are three things that come to mind: note taking, organisation, and practice. In biology, clear and concise notes, that are organised, are of paramount importance. In my opinion, study notes are a reflection of your mind, if they are messy and do not follow a proper structure, this will affect how you learn the content. Your knowledge of biology content will be broken and jumbled, and will most certainly contain gaps (but I will discuss this with some more examples further on). In terms of organisation, the advice I have just mentioned can apply with any subject. Planning how you study, what you study and when, at least a month in advance, can allow you to have a set timeline in which you achieve your goals. This removes the possibility of running out of time to study and cramming last minute, as well as ensuring a peace of mind when it comes to learning the overwhelming amount of biology content, as you will know you have an opportunity to cover it all in your schedule. Last but definitely not least, is practice! In my HSC examinations I walked into the Biology exam calm and confident. Why? Because I had drilled the whole syllabus, dot point back to front and upside down. I practiced and quizzed myself whenever I got the chance, whether I was on the bus, re-reading what we had gone over in class, or talking to my mum and dad about topics I had learnt about. By the time the last HSC study holiday begins, you should have practiced the content so much you could do it in your sleep. But this is only half the battle, and next comes the practicing of past papers, one after another! Can you see the common element? Repetition and practice. It will reinforce your learning as well as give you the confidence that comes with knowing your content well. Therefore, knowing you have done more than enough to drill the types of questions you could be asked.

3. The Foundation to Effective Study

The foundation to any effective study, biology or otherwise is good notes. As I have said above the key to setting your biology study on the right track for success is good notes. This means clear multi-coloured organised notes written in brief dot point form with headings, sub-headings, and even little footnotes or brackets, to provide extra clarity if needed. When I prepared for my HSC the two questions I would ask myself when looking at my notes were:

Can I see exactly what this page is about before reading it?

And

Do I know what part of the syllabus this is by just looking at it?

If the answer was "yes", my notes were obviously clear and ready to learn off, if not I would then ask myself what was confusing about them and make the necessary changes.

Here is an example of what my notes looked like for the Chemistry HSC. (Next page)

As you can see there are clear diagrams made with a ruler, clear labels, asterisks to further explain things I might find tricky later, and bullet point notes distinctly segregated into each syllabus dot point. Here we can see that these notes would be optimal to learn from, as they provide everything in a structured manner so that we can find what we need to with ease.

MORE REACTIVE METAL: L.E.O.A — LOOSE ELECTRONS OXIDATION ANODE

LESS REACTIVE METAL: G.E.R.C — GAIN ELECTRONS REDUCTION CATHODE

- IDENTIFY THE RELATIONSHIP BETWEEN DISPLACEMENT OF METAL IONS IN SOLUTION BY OTHER METALS TO THE RELATIVE ACTIVITY OF METALS

THE ABILITY OF SOME METALS TO GAIN OR LOSE ELECTRONS IS MEASURED ON THE ELECTROCHEMICAL SERIES

SERIES IS USEFUL BECAUSE IT BECOMES EASY TO PREDICT WHICH METAL WILL DISPLACE THE ION OF ANOTHER METAL.

IN DISPLACEMENT REACTIONS A MORE REACTIVE METAL WILL DISPLACE THE ION OF A LESS REACTIVE METAL FROM SOLUTION.

THE HIGHER A METAL IS ON THE STANDARD REDUCTIONS POTENTIAL TABLE, THE MORE REACTIVE IT IS.

EXAMPLE: Cu IN $Cu(NO_3)_2$
$Cu + (-1 \times 2) = 0, Cu - 2 = 0$
$Cu = +2$

OXIDATION STATE RULES:
Cl IN $HClO$
OXYGEN IS -2 IN A MOLECULE
$Cl + 1 - 2 = 0 \therefore Cl = +1$
HYDROGEN IS +1 IN A MOLECULE (EXCEPT HYDRIDES)
SINGLE IONS HAVE SAME OXIDATION NUMBER AS VALENCE NUMBER
OXIDATION NUMBER OF AN ELEMENT IS ZERO

EXAMPLES: DETERMINE WHETHER THESE ARE REDOX REACTIONS
$Mg + H_2SO_4 \longrightarrow MgSO_4 + H_2$ CHANGE IN OX. NO. = REDOX
$Mg \longrightarrow Mg^{2+} + 2e^-$ REACTION IS $H^+ \; 1^+ \longrightarrow 0$
$2H^+ + 2e^- \longrightarrow H_2$ (IF NO CHANGE, NOT A REDOX)

IN A REACTION IF OXIDATION NUMBER INCREASES THEN ELEMENT IS BEING OXIDISED
IN A REACTION IF OXIDATION NUMBER DECREASES THEN ELEMENT IS BEING REDUCED

(HSC Chemistry notes)

4. Preparation and Approaching the Scary Questions

One of the worst feelings as a student studying for the HSC is during the holidays. Study holidays! Having never confronted the notion of studying through an entire holiday it can be extremely daunting. It honestly would seem like a torturous experience for anyone looking at the prospect of having such a holiday. Which is why the most important skill I want to discuss when it comes to HSC preparation is making timetables. Timetables for me were like the 'holy grail' of studying. They provided everything for a demotivated student: the promise for an end date for study, an assurance that all necessary content will be covered before the exams, and finally that every day will have a plan already prepared with breaks, so that you will not become overwhelmed with the sheer volumes of work on a certain day. But when it comes to making timetables there is a technique that I believe is the most effective as we can see below:

TIME	MONDAY
8:00-9:00 AM	Breakfast
9:00-10:00 AM	Chemistry: Read through notes for topic 1
10:00-11:00 AM	Chemistry: Use palm cards to quiz self on topic 1 *Plus 30 min break*
11:00-12:00 AM	Chemistry: Use palm cards to quiz self on topic 1
12:00-1:00 PM	Lunch
1:00-2:00 PM	Biology: Read through notes for topic 1

2:00-3:00 PM	Biology: Use palm cards to quiz self on topic 1 *Plus 30 min break*
3:00-4:00 PM	Biology: Use palm cards to quiz self on topic 1
4:00-5:00 PM	Chemistry: Do a chemistry past paper (2016)
5:00-6:00 PM	Chemistry: Do a chemistry past paper (2016) *Plus 30 min break*
6:00-7:00 PM	Dinner
7:00-8:00 PM	Chemistry: Finish chemistry past paper
8:00-9:00 PM	Chemistry: Finish chemistry past paper *Plus 30 min review of chemistry notes*
9:00-10:00 PM	Biology: 30 min review of biology notes *Plus 30 min break*
10:30 PM	Relax for the rest of the evening

In my time tables I usually plan by hour so that a daily plan can be made that is more exact and detailed. This way you know exactly what you are doing and when, however you could also plan a timetable in blocs (i.e. a morning bloc, a midday/afternoon bloc and an evening bloc). This element of the timetable is flexible. However, the most important element to a timetable is that you have longer breaks not just for meals (thirty minute breaks at least). But also, quick five minute breaks for when you feel distracted or tired within those study blocs (these don't need to be noted in your timetable). Also, there should be a period at the end of the day which allows for review time to go over notes just to reinforce what you have covered during the day.

5. Answering scarier questions

The next idea I want to cover in this section is how to approach an HSC Biology past paper and especially those harder 8 marker exam questions near the end of the paper. When approaching an HSC paper there are a lot of different views as to how to approach the questions, and in what order to approach each section. My opinions regarding this section are subjective, however, in my experience I believe these methods to be the best based on my own results and study methods, those of my peers and those taught to me by my teachers. A biology paper consists of three sections: multiple choice, short answer questions, and an option which also consists of short answer questions. When starting a paper, I believe that it should be completed in order, multiple choice coming first. That said, the multiple-choice questions should be done carefully with deliberate emphasis placed on the wording of the questions. Especially in biology, very subtle word choice can change the implications of a question. This was always one of my biggest issues as a student. When looking at the biology multiple choice questions I always thought they were easy and could be rushed through. At times when I did past papers I would often skim read a question, tell myself that I knew what they were asking me and then jump on an answer, and quickly move onto the next question. This was a serious problem because I would often miss key subtleties in the question and lose several marks. I was so focused on rushing through the paper. In the Biology exam you will have more than enough time to complete the paper, with extra time to check over your answers. This means you can take a few minutes to read and circle key words in a multiple-choice question. In fact, I couldn't recommend doing this more highly! Circling key words in the question takes one second and helps reinforce what the question is actually asking you, whilst limiting the chance that you could misread or misinterpret the question. The next section in the paper is the short answer questions. They begin this section with 'lower order thinking' questions, such as identify the waste products in blood and how they are transported. These questions if you know your content, you will be able to do in your sleep, they are aimed at roughly band 4 level difficulty and should be completed with ease. However, as you move into the paper the questions becoming 'higher order thinking.' So, when approaching the harder and longer questions at the end of section two in the paper, I have a few techniques that will help remove the sense of panic and fear when you are confronted with a question in which you are unsure of what is being asking of you:

a. Circle the directive word

When looking at these larger 7-9 mark questions they will most definitely be in the band 6 level of difficulty. In knowing this, students need to understand that this is the place where they prove that they are capable of presenting a more complicated response. The first step is to identifying the directive word: is it **evaluate**, **discuss**, or **assess**? Once this is done we need to break down what each word really means. In almost every case the 'higher order' 7-9 mark questions have the directive word "evaluate" or "discuss" these both have different meanings.

"Evaluate" means that you must discuss the positives and the negatives of a biological concept and then finally make it very clear whether the positive elements outweigh the negative ones. To make this abundantly clear to the marker I always state from the outset that I have "evaluated" the pros and cons I have just explained in my response, and then state the phrase: "upon evaluation of these ideas it is clear that…" which is followed by the relevant ideas in the question

"Discuss" is a similar directive term, but differs from term evaluate (remember that to evaluate involves making a judgment of some kind after outlining and explaining the pros and cons of a biological topic). "Discuss" is a more neutral term, and does not involve making a judgment, so including one would be useless, and the marker would assess that you have not considered carefully enough the directive term of the question.

Finally, the term "assess" differs a little to the previous two terms evaluate and discuss. To assess involves identifying the key elements or reasons as to why a statement is correct or incorrect, and coming to an ultimate conclusion from this. For example, if a question asks to "Assess the importance of…" this means that that you need to state all the reasons why this concept is important or unimportant (chose one stance) and provide examples as to why this is true. Then this should be followed by a final statement along the lines of: "Based upon the evidence discussed it is clear that…"

b. Underline key terms from the syllabus

The next step is to figure out what part of the syllabus the question is targeting. The easiest way to do this is to underline what biological terms you can see in the question. For example, is it discussing the immune response, or meiosis or even evolution? Key words like "inheritance" or "Darwin" or even something as simple as "the human body" give us clues on what parts of the syllabus the question is targeting.

QUICK TIP: if you are ever unsure if a question is referring to a specific element in the syllabus or not, expand your answer to address more than one element, as markers will not remove marks for irrelevant information they will just ignore it which does no harm to you if you were incorrect and the information was not entirely relevant.

By now the question on the page should look something like this:

> *Assess the importance* of the work of *Beadle and Tatum* to the ability to produce a specific *transgenic species.*
>
> (Biology sample question)

c. Make a plan of your response

Before you rush into writing straight away after completing the first two steps, it is important to make a quick plan in dot points of what you want to cover. On the side of the page (or even in a spare writing booklet), quickly jot down your judgement (if needed) on a question as well as the main points, in order of relevance that you want to cover. This ensures that your writing will be structured and clear to follow for the marker, and clarity is always an easy road to quick marks.

Advice and Last Minute Tips

When looking back at my experiences with the HSC, I cannot stress enough how important it is to have a positive mindset towards exams. I went into my first exam terrified and on the verge of tears. That mindset was poisonous and I believe it greatly affected my performance in my English exam. So, to help future students from forming a toxic approach to exams, here are my last-minute tips for the night before the exam, and exam day itself. The night before the exam should not be the time for cramming or frantically doing past papers but rather should remain as an opportunity to read through notes and look over any summaries to reinforce last minute concepts. Another important rule I have is to never stay up late, it is much more productive to get enough sleep so you can stay alert for the next day rather than trying to overload your brain with information. Moving on to the exam day itself, I would start by having a solid breakfast, and talking to a friend or family member in order to be calm and help ground yourself. I would not look through notes as any study would be useless at this point of time and would serve only as a means to cause stress, especially if you stumbled across a concept that you did not understand. In my case, I would talk to my mother before my exam for reassurance and then listen to some music or talk to a friend before I went in.

For all students facing these exams soon the last piece of advice I can give is to trust in yourself and the study you have done. If you are reading this now, know that you obviously have a drive and passion to do well in your studies and if you approach your exams calmly and with a positive mindset you can and will achieve your HSC and secondary education goals.

BUSINESS STUDIES AND GENERAL TIPS FROM FIRST IN THE STATE

By Tim Yang

> *"Nothing is impossible, the word itself says 'I'm possible'"*
> *– Audrey Hepburn*

Hey there! I'm Tim and I am very glad that you have taken the initiative to read my article about getting an idea on how you can come first in the state for HSC Business Studies! You see, many students simply jump right into studying, without figuring out the correct and most effective learning techniques first. Because of this reason, they may limit their academic potential. It is great that you are trying to improve on how you learn! And speaking of learning, I can tell you that this is one of the most valuable skills the HSC has taught me. Knowing how to productively learn will help you transition quickly into the workplace, and obtain new skills that are in high demand, and most importantly, help you become a better version of yourself. Before we get onto some tips and tricks, I would like to share with you my HSC journey, so you can avoid the mistakes that I made and learn from my experiences.

My Business Studies Journey

Contrary to what many may believe, my HSC Business studies journey began with a dramatic error rather than success! I had dropped sixteen ranks from year eleven after the first year twelve Business internal assessment task. Initially, the shock significantly demotivated me from studying Business. My mind was full of self-resentment and anxiety. I kept asking myself, "how was I going to get to Band 6 for Business Studies this year?" You see, my school's ranking was and is still quite average compared to other schools overall in NSW. This meant I had to score very high in internal rankings to even have a chance at achieving an aggregate Band 6 Mark for business studies. The long story short, my chances for recovering my internal ranks were slim to none, and so was my chance in getting that Band 6. This realisation was made worse because in the previous year's Business cohort, no one had achieved Band 6! I needed at least a Band 6 for Business to get a high enough ATAR to get into the course I desired. What was I going to do now?

Well, I didn't lose all hope, as the old adage goes, "There is always light at the end of the tunnel, and you just have to keep going", and "keep going" was exactly what I did. The terrible mark I received in my first Business assessment was like an alarm bell that propelled me into developing a more serious attitude towards studying the subject. I began doing more past paper questions, writing more essays and business reports. I began asking for more feedback from teachers; inquiring into the fine details of the syllabus that rarely any student would care about. But I didn't just do the past papers. I actually ensured they were 'double marked' so that I could clearly identify any improvements I could make. I did this by marking them myself, and then handing it to a teacher for feedback. The double benefit of marking the past paper yourself is that you get to see your answers from the perspective of a HSC marker, and thus understand how to avoid losing unnecessary marks. To put it bluntly, it's like you are becoming 'one' with the sample answers and marking criteria that you use to mark your own responses.

Doing these tasks in order to get better was difficult at first, as they ate into a significant portion of my study time. However, as I practised more, they became easier. From my learning experience I had created a new systematic way to study, and understand Business Studies, and score well on exams. I was surprised that my system had worked so well! I discovered that I had received full-marks on my mid-course exam following my dreadful first term mark. Full marks indeed! It was something that hadn't been done for more than a decade at my school. Through this change in my studying method, my ranking shot up to first place. I was now even more driven to improve my Business Skills than ever before. From then on, I was able to maintain first place for all of my other internals. This enabled me to secure first place overall at the end of the year for Business Studies. I now had a fighting chance to State-rank this subject!

Then of course, you know how the rest of the story went. But the truth be told, I did not know I was going to get first rank in the State for Business Studies, until the very moment the premier of New South Wales, Gladys Berejiklian, called me on a cloudy Friday morning; while I was lazily eating my breakfast cereal to notify me of my achievement. I guess the overarching lesson you can all learn here is to always stay determined until you have achieve your goal, and always stay humble afterwards. This was something I told myself nearly every time I headed into an exam room.

Tips I value the most for effective learning

If you feel like you are, or will be, in the situation that I was in, you need to ensure you have a 'growth mindset.' "What is a growth mindset? And Why should I get this mindset?" you may ask. Well, if you have a 'growth mindset' you will strive towards continuous improvement, and believe that you can get better, and constantly evaluate yourself to see which areas you can improve on. This mindset is crucial in getting closer to full marks in the HSC. You need to understand every single syllabus dot point inside and out, and be able to write concise and coherent business reports, and be able to analyse hypothetical situations adeptly. The most valuable feature of having this mindset is that it makes you resilient to failure. You will begin to see that every mistake you made and corrected is one step closer to your success. This resilience towards making errors was what helped me get out of that dreadful situation, and for that reason, you should also adopt a 'growth mindset.'

My second tip for you is to ensure you get enough sleep! It does not matter whether you are staying up till two in the morning to study for a test held the next day, or to binge watch YouTube/Netflix, if you want to *ace* HSC you should have been sound asleep before then! As school should start around 8:30 am, you need to be asleep by the latest 12 am each night, to get that adequate eight hours of sleep (depending on how long it takes for you to travel to school, you may have to sleep even earlier). And before an exam, you should sleep even more! I actually had around nine hours of sleep the night before almost all of my exams. The reason why you should sleep well is that it helps you absorb new content and skills that you learnt during the day. Indeed, individuals who slept well had over a 40% higher memory retention ability than those who were sleep deprived according to one study (Walker, 2008). Sleeping better before exams will give you an edge over the majority of your peers (by making you feel less stressed and more refreshed), who likely did not sleep well from over-studying the night before. So, my tip here is: sleep well, feel well, and you'll do well.

Tips specific to Business Studies

1. DO NOT UNDERESTIMATE Business Studies (BS)

If you think that Business Studies contains just general knowledge, and that memorising the syllabus is enough to guarantee you a Band 6 in the HSC, you are WRONG! Teachers can 'smell' that attitude from just looking at the executive summary in your reports, and from looking at the first sentence of your short answer questions, and they will punish you. Therefore, ensure you understand the details of the Syllabus as well.

Here is an example on the topic of Operations: The strategy of supply management requires the business to manage its E-commerce related sourcing through E-procurement, that is a system that allows suppliers to directly access a business' information via online means. Through E-procurement systems, the supplier can automatically replete a business' stock rather than through the traditional repletion method of the business filing orders for stock. This increases the business' volume flexibility, and lowers warehousing costs as fewer stocks need to be kept at the one time (stock is filled automatically). Through helping ensure inventory levels are adequate, E-procurement also lowers the chance of being out of stock, which can delay customer purchase orders, and so result in customer dissatisfaction. Having stated this information, you can link all of the positive points about E-Commerce to the strategic role of operations (i.e. cost leadership and goods/service differentiation), and how it helps operations achieve strategic objectives (in this case: flexibility and speed - you may also know them as performance objectives, which is an operations strategy itself).

The above example demonstrates that all those points come from just the one sub-dot point: E-Commerce under Supply Chain Management! This is the kind of understanding you will need to TOP

THE STATE! So, don't underestimate Business Studies, or else it will crush you hard.

2. USE CASE STUDIES

If you do not use case studies you will NOT get a Band 6! Section IV of the HSC business studies exam require you write an essay, or business report based on one topic of the syllabus that is supported by real-life examples/case studies. For example, you can use Qantas as a case study to support your arguments to an operations question such as: "Evaluate: the effectiveness of operations strategies can help a business respond to its external influences."

For this question, you must to use some data regarding Qantas' relating to operational performance in order to evaluate its operational strategies. Accordingly, we can only say Qantas' quality management is effective in ensuring aircraft safety and thus the quality of its flights (a customer expectation), only if it has a good safety record. Qantas does have a perfect safety record (no major accidents). On considering this evaluation, we can say Qantas' quality management methods, such as quality control in the form having engineers check the planes' electronic and mechanical systems before take-off are effective. Therefore you need to be as detailed as possible when using a case study to support your argument. Don't just identify the statistic, and then say some strategy is effective, describe the strategy as well! For example: Qantas' has been using established technologies (the strategy) such as electronic bag tags, and an online check-in system (how the strategy is used by the case study business), which lowers labour costs; this has helped Qantas effectively lower its overall costs (the objective and evaluation) by seven billion dollars in the last thirteen years (further statistical evidence)

Note: You don't need to include too many statistics in your extended responses- unlike for Economics. Of course, you can include statistics, as long as they support your argument. For example, statistics may be appropriate to include if you are trying to show improvements in certain Business KPIs to substantiate, for example, the effectiveness of certain business strategies.

3. LINK THE SYLLABUS POINTS

Each syllabus dot point should not be considered in Isolation. Many dot points are related. For example, you can link dot points by showing how a business functions' strategies improve its processes, and/or also helps the function achieve its strategic role.

Here is an example regarding the strategic role: The marketing strategy of personal selling helps create long-term customer relationships. This means that in repeated sales, the salesperson and the customer can develop a personal connection. It delivers a more individualised and enticing message to customers, which can also lead to more sales and perhaps profit. For these reasons, the promotional strategy of personal selling helps the marketing function achieve its strategic role of realising profit maximisation.

Regardless of your current ranks and marks, just remember that you need to believe in yourself first to achieve the goal ATAR that you want. There are a lot of tips to take in, and each of them will take some effort to master. No matter how bad things get, know that there are always other pathways for you to get into your dream university course. When you're not studying, make sure to hang out with your friends and family from time-to-time. The HSC is not your whole life in this coming year, but merely a part of it.

Thank you for reading, and good luck with the HSC!

Yazhou (Tim) Yang

PHYSICS: IS THERE ARE DREAM TOO BIG?

By Jesse Wright

> "I am and always will be the optimist, the hoper of far-flung hopes and the dreamer of improbable dreams." – The Doctor

Who is this person?

My name is Jesse Wright and I am from Mount Saint Patrick College (Murwillumbah) a small-medium sized school from NSW. I began completing HSC subjects in Year 10 (2016) and finished the HSC in 2018 with an ATAR of 99.85. I was ranked 4th in the state for Physics in 2018.

I have always loved Science, Maths, and general problem solving. My most vivid childhood memory is staring up, admiringly at my father as he placed a folded note in my palm. On it was a tiny clue, my ticket to adventure; 'A place where you find the alphabet.' A dictionary maybe?... But that's not a place. Wait! The alphabet? A place where you find letters... The letterbox! After hours of running from lead to lead around my property, I found myself plucking a sheet from the underside of my treehouse. From it, numbers and symbols jumped at me, begging to be solved. This was the type of challenge I had come to live for. From that moment, I felt my parents wonder for the world filling me, igniting an undying yearning to understand it. At home, extensive discussion of STEM breakthroughs has inspired me to explore my own ideas, which I hope to implement in the future.

My constantly active mind will most likely land you in some weird and wonderful conversations with me. Whilst I dislike small talk; if you start discussing science, technology, social structure, Doctor Who or any other enthralling topic I will soak up your thoughts before excitedly rambling in an overly gesticulated manner for hours on end (my old debating friends can attest to this - many a time I have been caught in a wild discussion or explanation only to see in the corner of my eye someone mirroring my extreme hand movements).

Personally, I believe that goal setting, and a little blind optimism is key to success. This applies both to the HSC and life in general. I spoke about this in my Dux speech earlier this year.

Excerpt from Dux Speech

Six years ago, I remember being where many year 7 students are today, staring up at a completely unfamiliar face blabbering on about some foreign set of exams called the HSC. Whilst I didn't know exactly what they were talking about, something about the sense of excitement and accomplishment in the voice I was hearing planted a seed in my mind. One day I wanted to be up there. One day I wanted to give that speech.

When I first received my ATAR, many people said that I must be some sort of 'genius' as it is the first time our school had received a score over 99.40 in its 50+ year history. But let me tell you now, that's simply not true. The only reason I have achieved any of my goals is because I have absolutely worked my butt off to get here. In the last few years, I dedicated almost every second I could to revising topics, crunching through past papers and tirelessly editing English scripts.

So, in order to achieve your best results, I urge you, *dare* to dream and *dare* to pursue it!

Personally, I have always dreamed of attending some of America's top universities. I know only a small percentage of international applicants are accepted, most of which have far more outstanding credentials than myself. Yet, I have dared to dream, and because of this goal, and others like it, I have done well in the HSC.

When I broke this dream into 'micro' goals, I realised that I would need high HSC marks (as well as US SAT tests which cover similar content). This pushed me in my second week of term two holiday study to finish that 'next' physics past paper; to do one more edit of my English essays and to harass Mr Hoy for one more book of maths questions.

Coming from a rural area, it is easy to get caught up in the idea that high achieving students are only a product of expensive private schools in Sydney. I wasn't sure if I would get a Band 6 in Physics, let alone get a State ranking. In no way was getting there easy, but it was also in no way impossible.

So just aim as high as you can, do the best you can, and you might just surprise yourself with what you can do.

Past Papers - The strategy

My approach to past papers varied greatly depending on the subject, here is a brief outline of the strategy I used:

After finishing each physics dot point in the syllabus, I would complete questions pertaining to that dot point. I would start with easy, low mark questions and then check the marking criteria to ensure I had covered all the content. Once I was consistently getting full marks on these types of questions, I would move on to complete 5-8 mark questions. Firstly, I would mark these myself using the marking guidelines before getting these questions double marked by my teacher (who has also worked as an HSC marker). Receiving this teacher input is imperative as they will pick up errors, such as the coherence of the answer that students would never have noticed.

The syllabus - your friend, but also your foe

Throughout the HSC you will most likely hear something akin to 'the Syllabus is your new Bible - Worship It.' This document provides a great starting point to ensure you have covered and understood the topics of the course. However, in 2018, NESA decided to throw in some curveballs across many subjects (in a way that I imagine pre-empts the new exams of 2019). The following 6-mark question from the HSC physics paper required primarily preliminary content in terms of understanding circuits in order to answer well. I also benefited from knowledge not covered in the syllabus which had been acquired from studying for the SAT entrance exams for US universities (much of this content has been incorporated into the 2019 syllabus).

Sample question:

> *The amounts of energy, voltage and current used by the electrical distribution system vary greatly throughout the day as differing amounts of load are applied to the grid. Use your knowledge of Physics to explain these changes at each point on the electrical distribution system.*

For this particular question, most students would have answered this question with the understanding the $P_{loss} = I^2R$, a concept drilled in throughout the past HSC course. However, few understood the changes to voltage and current following the power loss, and the effect of the parallel circuits between the houses. I on the other hand, was able to write up far beyond the word limit due to this extra detail of knowledge. Whilst it is important to be as concise as possible in giving answers, in this example, there was simply a large amount of content that was being assessed and needed to be discussed.

Another aspect of the syllabus that your teachers must cover in assessments are 'Prescribed Focus Areas.' A lot of questions are taken from this part of the document. Have your teacher get you a copy or find it yourself, it is a great resource to study and many students are not told about it, or at least do not find out about it until later in the year.

Problem Solving

This is another area in which it is vital to step beyond the limitations of the syllabus and really explore your understanding of Physics. Doing Extension Maths courses will certainly give you an upper hand, to this day I do not truly understand the standard method used to solve projectile motion in physics as I found the method taught in Mathematics more intuitive and easier to work with. Whenever you have a spare 10 or 15 minutes I urge you to play around with your physics formulae and see what interesting results you can derive or relationships you can see. Perhaps you can think of an interesting question or problem that you need to solve which uses multiple concepts or formulae.

I found that doing these kinds of things was vital to helping me answer Q28b of my HSC paper (no other students from my school were able to solve this question.

> *The earth has mass 6×10^{24} kg and radius 6371km. If, hypothetically, a 2-tonne rocket is launched vertically from the surface of the earth at 50km/s, what will its velocity be when it is 100km from the ground. *Hint, you will first need to calculate the Gravitational Potential Energy of the rocket at 100km above the surface of the earth.*

Most people who have covered the content on energy will be able to solve part *a* fairly easily. However, part *b*, required students to use the equation for GPE to then calculate kinetic energy, and in turn velocity. Because we had to use 2 or 3 equations to solve this, most students were unable to see what had to be done and thus you need to practise playing with equations, so you are able to work out what to do.

Sample answer:

Initial potential energy of mass

$$E_{pi} = -\frac{GMm}{r} = \frac{-6.67 \times 10^{-11} \times 7.35 \times 10^{22} \times 20}{1.74 \times 10^6}$$

$$= -5.64 \times 10^7 \text{ J}$$

Final potential energy of mass

$$E_{pf} = \frac{-6.67 \times 10^{-11} \times 7.35 \times 10^{22} \times 20}{2.24 \times 10^6}$$

$$= -4.38 \times 10^7 \text{ J}$$

$$\Delta E_p = E_{pf} - E_{pi} = 1.26 \times 10^7 \text{ J}$$

(Sample answer)

Extended Responses

I found extended responses to be one of the most difficult parts of HSC physics where I could lose several marks for any given question (this happened right up until the trial examinations). Some of my biggest problems included providing irrelevant information, giving incoherent answers, or misunderstanding the intention of the question. The most important thing to do with such questions is to ensure that you immediately give a succinct answer to the question (similar to a thesis in English) to show the markers that you know exactly what you are talking about. I would also ensure you do a scaffold at the top of your question with all information you wish to talk about as this will be marked if you forget to write something later on. Do not forget that tables can be a great way to answer questions (I did this in the last question for Medical Physics in the HSC).

Unfortunately, beyond this, there is no shortcut and secret. You just need to practise hundreds of these responses and get your teacher to mark as many as possible.

Note-taking

Throughout Year 12 I had 2 physics notebooks. The first I used for general note-taking within class, solving example problems and writing down experimental data. I tried to fit all content I was being taught, and all information I could possibly need (even if it was slightly outside of the syllabus) into this text. The second book was structured such that each page covered one dot point from the physics syllabus. I found this integral to ensuring that I knew exactly what content fell under each dot point, so I could cover everything needed for all dot point questions in exams. I would usually try and cover most content before class, and add to this book after the lesson. This way I also knew what content I needed to study more, as usually this was what I had missed in my initial round of note-taking.

Study

My primary mode of note taking was the use of past papers which I have discussed above. This way I was always covering a variety of topics and ensuring that I could answer the question. Another method that I also used in other science subjects was to have my parents read the dot point in my second summary book and then I would try and recall most of the content on the page. They would then ask me questions about any points that I missed, and I would highlight this information to review later.

Timetabling

An important thing is to make sure that the HSC does not consume you. During 2018, I still did a lot of volunteer work and paid work, whilst taking on many roles such as school captain within my High School. If you are like me, and feel that you need to be constantly studying through the HSC, these activities provide the perfect opportunity to give your brain a break and to let you do something else for a while.

I also found it crucial to get decent sleep during the HSC. Many people used to ask me how I was able to achieve as much as I could in a day. The key is that a well-rested mind is far more productive, and able to learn a great deal more than one that is deprived of sleep.

Here is a typical day for me:

TIME	ACTIVITY
7:30-8:30 AM	Wake up/get ready for school
8:45-3:15 PM	School
3:30-5:00 PM	Paid and/or volunteer work
5:00-6:00 PM	Study
6:00-7:00 PM	Dinner and TV
7:00-9:30 PM	Study
9:30 PM	Sleep

One of the major mistakes that I made was not leaving enough time for myself to rest and recover. At the time of my half yearlies, I almost burnt out and bombed my exams as a result of taking on too many commitments, including taking on an extra university course that was not related to my schooling. Step back and make sure to give yourself breaks when needed.

What should I do in holidays?

I found that using my holidays effectively was invaluable to enabling my success. I think the most important things is to try and cover a lot of content and concepts before you do them in class. This way, your time with your teacher will reinforce each concept and ensure you have a good understanding. This will also allow you to ask more deep and insightful questions instead of having to say, 'can you please repeat that?' Whilst I only used textbooks when doing this for Maths, Edrolo, HSC hub and HSC study lab, these were vital to get ahead in Physics.

TEAMWORK!

Whilst a lot of the HSC is being able to sit down and put in the hard yards, collaborating with your friends can make the year a heck of a lot easier. In Physics, friends and I would constantly be bouncing ideas off one another, challenging each other's understanding of concepts and pushing each other to do better through competition, this was perhaps at times a little too intense.

English was one of my weaker subjects, so this is where I found the help of those more literary-minded invaluable. Over the course of the year my peers must have seen more than a hundred drafts of all my essays - your teachers simply don't have the time to do this for each individual student.

Don't forget the teachers

I cannot emphasise this enough, teachers are your best friends. Whether it is after school tutorials, marking past papers or just providing you with general coaching & support, these guys put an exceptional amount of effort into you. Therefore be grateful, and make sure you take advantage of any help they are willing to give you.

Love your subjects!

In the time I find for myself, whether it be 15 minutes between commitments or hours late at night, I, by reflex, open a new tab and search out MITopencourseware, Crash Course or Kahn academy. Within seconds I am entranced in a world of math, physics or programming, and a wave of serenity washes over me. If no laptop is nearby, I sometimes turn to inventing my own intriguing mathematical problems, or I explore the tantalizing realms of number theory. I also indulge in literature such as Brian Greene's 'The Elegant Universe,' to understand nature's patterns and obtain unadulterated joy. It is important to find what you love about your study, even if it is not always syllabus based. This excitement will make your study more enjoyable and productive as you can truly engage with the content you are covering.

MODERN HISTORY

by Zoe Zhang

> *"If you think you have it tough, read history books."* – Bill Maher

Hi everyone! If you're reading this, then you probably chose Modern History, or are thinking of choosing it for your HSC year. I really enjoyed the subject which provided me with some motivation during exams. If you like the subject, you won't regret taking it.

Surviving the HSC

Throughout my whole HSC year, the advice I generally received from friends, families and teachers was *'Don't stress too much*, the HSC is not the end of the world' and the hypothetically encouraging *'There is a life after the HSC'*.

I despised that advice!

In year 12 I had the mindset that the HSC was my life and it was imperative that I did well in it to succeed in life after the HSC. Putting things into perspective now, I agree wholeheartedly with the advice I was given earlier. However, I know from experience that it is hard to distance yourself from the all-seeming importance of writing, perfecting and memorising 50 Modern History essays to get good marks in exams (I'm not kidding, there were a lot of syllabus dot points).

I found Modern History to be the most stressful of my subjects because of its high workload and numerous essays. However, it was also my favourite as it was actually very interesting. The content covered dictators, poo sticks and manipulative personalities providing a stimulating break from English and Maths related subjects. However, studying Modern History also forced me to become more critical when analysing sources, events and people which enabled me to improve my essay writing skills and ability to form logical arguments.

So to conclude a post-HSC perspective, I would say the HSC is just a speed bump in your life. It was an uncomfortable ride, one I wouldn't want to repeat (once was more than enough). I stressed a lot, cried and got minimal sleep but I did learn from the experience.

Time Management Strategies

School Term

I definitely spent a large portion of my study time on Modern History. From the beginning of Year 12, I knew I only wanted to study 10 units in school which would allow me more time to focus on my subjects while also having enough leisure time to relax (sleep).

Personally, I never followed a strict study timetable. Instead, I would plan for each week or day by allocating time (usually 1-2 hours) to do assignments, essay plans or homework based on their urgency.

TIP 1: Prioritisation

While it can be tempting to focus on subjects we like, it is extremely important that you stay on top of all your assignments and homework, because even if you do extremely well in one subject, a poor mark in another can drag your overall performance down.

To help prioritise your tasks, I would recommend drawing yourself up a to-do-list or table. You can do this on your laptop (Onenote, Sticky Notes etc.) or physically on paper. Personally, I liked to type up a huge *to-do-list* for each of my subjects including homework, assignments and exam preparation. Everything I would like to have achieved before an assessment block went onto a *to-do-list*.

Note: Ranking tasks based on urgency helps you keep track of what you need to prioritise.

Then, I would write the tasks I wanted to complete that day on paper which helped break down the things I had to do. It also made my list look more manageable and less overwhelming while giving me motivation when I physically crossed out a task I had completed.

TIP 2: Take Breaks to Keep Yourself Sane

When I did plan out my day, I would block out time to eat, shower, relax and sleep which was important to keep my study plan realistic, and make sure I did not burn myself out. Also, I made sure I gave myself 20-30 minutes to wind down after I came home from school which I usually used to shower, watch *Youtube* or read before I resumed studying.

TIP 3: Don't be afraid of procrastination

Procrastination is every student's worse enemy. It always starts with just one *Youtube* video, five minutes of social media, or a 10 minute nap before you find that 2 hours have gone by and you still haven't finished your English study notes, and that familiar feeling of dread, shame and self-hatred creeps up on you. You tell yourself that you will never procrastinate again, and that you'll spend the next 5 hours purely studying to make up for lost time. This is not realistic, as it would push you closer to a burn-out. Procrastination ends up being a reoccurring fact of life.

You don't have to avoid procrastination forever (or until the end of exams). Instead, fit it into your allocated break times and set a timer to ensure that you don't overly exceed the time limit you set yourself.

Finally, even if you do end up procrastinating outside your break times, DON'T fall into the cycle of self-hatred and shame that will demoralise you, and disrupt your study plan. Instead, catch yourself before you spend too long streaming online, or liking Facebook posts; remind yourself why you need to study and what you still have to do. This really helps prompt you to revaluate the time you have left and prevent a note cramming session before exams.

TIP 4: Sleep

Although you may not have to wake up early the next morning to go to school, and can technically sleep and wake up whenever you want; I strongly recommend against pulling all-nighters and waking up at 5pm the next day.

Sleep is extremely important for a healthy, functioning body and an active mind. Getting enough sleeps everyday boosts productivity and the amount of information you retain from studying.

TRY NOT to rely on caffeine because it is a temporary boost of energy which might end up in a 'crash' or drastic energy drop later in the day (caffeine 'crashes' certainly did happen for me). Even if this does not happen to you, I would not depend on it during an exam.

TRY to get 8-10 hours of sleep a day. It really does make a difference on general wellbeing and study productivity.

TIP 5: Stress and Motivation

Stress is a normal part of the HSC experience. The advice, "don't stress," felt completely irrelevant to me. Instead, I would recommend you accept it and find a way to limit or use it.

HSC life shouldn't always be about studying - spend time with family and friends.

Studying 24/7 every day of the holidays is impossible. Instead, it is important to fit in leisure time such as eating dinner with the family, going to birthday parties, or even watching a movie. Having conversations with family and friends about anything (I usually complained about exams and study loads) was a great way for me to destress and keep myself from burning out.

About Modern History

Studying Modern History is stressful! There is a lot of memorising, as well as laborious reading and essay writing. However, it was the most interesting subject I took in high school and incredibly rewarding as it taught me essential critical thinking and analysis skills.

What I would do differently:

I **used to** make notes for modern history by reading through resources, highlighting chunks of information then typing up summarised notes on my laptop. However, this was time-consuming and I usually did not end up using all my notes. Actually, only around 30-50% of my notes were actually used in writing essay plans.

So, while I was putting together a study guide for somebody I was tutoring, I came across some useful note-taking tips while browsing online:

- Read each chapter, bookmark sections with information you think is important (or highlight)
- At the end of each section, type up relevant pieces of information (bullet point form makes it easier to read)
    - Start forming arguments - organise thematically
    - Add substance to arguments (quotes, details)

Achieving Results in Modern History

There are a few things you must do to succeed in history:

- READ: resources given by your teachers from historians, Access to History and HTA are vital to success in Modern History as they give you the knowledge foundation to answer short answer questions and build essay plans.
    - o This is where you get your notes, quotes and details from.
- MAKE NOTES: Create notes for each module:
    - o Breaking information into bullet point form makes it more easily digestible when you are studying.
    - o Include quote banks and details.
- WRITE ESSAY PLANS: Start as early as possible because you have a lot to get through:
    - o Make essay questions by putting 'Assess' in front of the syllabus dot points and create a full plan to answer these (including introduction, lines of arguments and conclusion).
    - o This also enables you organise your thoughts on the topic into logical arguments. (Refer to one of my essay plans).
- GET FEEDBACK: Send essay plans to your teacher to ensure you're on the right track, and get feedback on where you need to improve. It's a constant back-and-forth process so don't expect perfection from your first draft:
    - o For me, this was one of the most important contributors to my success.
- FIX ESSAYS: Revise over your teacher's feedback and implement advice given.

Notes and Organisation

At the end of the note-taking process I had PAGES of notes (30+ for WWI) to go through during exam preparation, which was extremely tedious. I ended up filtering through my notes and making a summarised version for the WWI section; where the exam questions were mostly short answer. For the other modules (National Study, Personality, Peace and Conflict) I used my essay plans as study resources during exam preparation.

The syllabus is **EXTREMELY** important for Modern History, as exam short answer and essay questions are created from them. I would recommend organising your notes under syllabus dot points to make it easier to write essay plans. Notes for the essay-based modules should be completed early on and structured by syllabus dot points. Including quotes and analysis by historians to make it easier to write essay plans.

Example Essay Plan

To what extent was the Great Depression responsible for the collapse of the Weimar Republic?

Breakdown of key terms – do this in your plan	Responsibility: cannot be wholly responsible, all factors intertwined

1. Direct response to the directive and question 'to what extent was responsible' 2. Follow through of my thesis 3. Line of argument 1 4. Line of argument 2 5. Line of argument 3	Sample introduction The Great Depression held significant responsibility₁ as a catalyst for the collapse of the Weimar Republic as it created the extreme socio-economic conditions which exacerbated underlying issues plaguing the Republic from its formation.₂ The Great Depression, instigated by the Wall Street Crash in October 1929 exposed the Republic's inability to maintain social support and generate sustainable economic solutions₃, enabling the transition from economic to political crisis₄ which engendered its collapse. However, fundamental failures of the Republic₅ which enabled such disastrous conditions of the Great Depression can be traced back to its inability to obtain genuine support for democracy, aggravated by its incomplete changeover from autocracy which allowed residual conservative powers to consistently act as an undermining force.
1. Topic sentence: point of the paragraph which supports your thesis. 2. Restating thesis and answer to the question – makes it clear to the marker that you are ANSWERING THE QUESTION 3. Point → explain→detail 4. Use of bullet points in essay plans make it easier for study 5. Link back to thesis and question	Sample body paragraph Fundamentally, the Great Depression exposed underlying failures of the Republic and created the extreme socio-economic conditions₁ which enabled the political collapse of democracy, affirming the significant extent of its responsibility as a catalyst to the Republic's collapse₂. - Instigated by the Wall Street Crash in October 1929, unravels short-term success of Stresemann's Dawes Plan 1924 which provided loans of 800 million marks from the USA₃ ○ Wall Street Crash₄, recalling of loans: failure of Republic in funding economically unsustainable projects such as parks, schools and long-term schemes i.e. Unemployment Insurance Act 1927 - Widespread social discontent destabilised Republic – led to collapse₅

6. Historian quotes can add sophistication 7. Short reference to syllabus dot point not included in the question can show depth of your analysis and understanding of the topic 8. Concluding statement should restate the thesis and point of the paragraph 9. Historian quotes can also be used to support your argument while adding eloquence to your essay	○ National income was 39% less that it had been in 1929 and increase in unemployment from 2 million in 1929 to 6 million in 1933 ○ Extensive social welfare policy was rendered obsolete i.e. Unemployment Insurance Act which could only support 800,000 individuals ○ Initial progressive social reforms dominantly served to increase public expectations of the state which resulted in severe disappointment and disillusionment when government unable to maintain reforms ○ Increasing crime and declining 'morality' – decreasing confidence in ability of Weimar to maintain social stability, psychological damage • Considerable discontent exploited by enemies of Republic in form of effective propaganda ○ "youthful dynamism" (Evans)$_6$ of Hitler and the NSDAP sowed widespread mistrust of Republic • Voters increasingly demonstrated preference for extremist parties of both right and left, facilitating rise of Nazi party$_7$ • 1930 elections, NSDAP increased vote from 810,000 to 6.4 million accounting for 18.3% of electorate and becoming second largest political party Thus, the Great Depression held significant responsibility in the Republic's collapse as it exacerbated underlying failures to create the extreme conditions facilitating political collapse$_8$ affirming 'Whatever the intrinsic political weaknesses of Weimar democracy…it was undoubtedly the Depression which precipitated the actual collapse of Weimar democracy…$_9$' [Fullbrook].

	SAMPLE CONCLUSION
1. Transition word indicating conclusion 2. Restate thesis but try to reword so it is not the exact same as the introduction 3. Summarise points supporting your thesis (line of arguments)	<u>Ultimately</u>$_1$, the <u>Great Depression held significant responsibility for the collapse of the Weimar Republic in its role as a catalyst</u>$_2$. By <u>uncovering the Republic's underlying economic and political instability and triggering subsequent political intrigue, the Great Depression accelerated the final demise of democracy.</u>$_3$

Exam Preparation

Writing essay plans early on certainly helps lighten the workload and stress when approaching exams, especially as they will form the bulk of your study resources (avoid stress-cramming because it is NOT effective).

Once I had my collection of essay plans (each question made by putting 'assess' in front of the syllabus dot points as I mentioned earlier, and also essay questions from past papers), I would rewrite them on paper under timed conditions and in full essay format (complete sentences, not bullet points).

Why did I do this?

- Allowed me to plan out my time during exams since I discovered how much I could write under time constraints:
    - Allocate strict time limit for each part of the essay(i.e. introduction, bodies and conclusion).
- To improve the legibility of my handwriting:
    - Markers **do** need to know what you've written to give you marks.

- Helped me memorise key points, expressions and quotes which really helped me during exams as I had something to fall back on during mind blanks.
- Constant practice increased my writing speed.

Exam Techniques

Reading time:

- In 5 minute reading time, read over all your sources and short answer questions.
- Plan out your responses to the short answer questions so you minimise time used to think over your answers:
    o Gives you more time for other sections
- I did not read the essay questions in the reading time. It was a personal choice as I did not want to be distracted from the first short answer section.

Short answer questions:

- Make sure you **answer the question**:
    o This is obvious but a lot of people tend to fill up space with information they memorised even if it's irrelevant to the question
- The amount of marks allocated to the question provides a guide on how much you need to write:
    o E.g. 2 marks – give 2 examples.
- This section is your chance to save time for essay-based sections so don't spend too long on each question:
    o Make sure you leave yourself a sufficient amount of time for the next sections, so don't get bogged down writing for 2 or 3 mark questions

Essays

- **Don't** panic if the essay question is not what you wanted it to be.
- Identify **key terms** and **directives**:
    - This will guide your response.
    - Each part of your essay should constantly deal with the question.
- **Plan** out a thesis and line of arguments to answer the set question:
    - General knowledge, detail and facts you have studied should be in your head (you will be surprised by how much you remember).
- **Don't** just write down an essay you have memorised:
    - It is very clear to the marker when you start writing about things irrelevant to the question.
    - You are not going to get in the top range if you don't **answer the question.**
- While writing, keep a note on how much time you have left:
    - The general time limit for an essay is 45 minutes, this is a loose guide:
        - 5 minutes plan.
        - 5 minutes introduction.
        - 10 minutes for each body paragraph (usually 3 but depends on the question).
        - 5 minutes conclusion.
    - Most of the time, I would have 1 minute for the conclusion but that would be enough for me to finish the essay.

Have a Conclusion

- It is so easy to run out of time for a conclusion for essays in the exam, but it is IMPORTANT that you have one as it gives it **cohesion** and structure (part of the marking criteria).
- If you know you won't have time for one if you continue writing your body paragraph, STOP:
    o Try to end the paragraph as neatly as possible and WRITE A CONCLUSION!

Final tips and advice

1. Keep yourself healthy:
    - Take exercise breaks and maintain a healthy lifestyle (sleep well, and eat a balanced diet).
2. Take it one step at a time, and remember to breathe. Don't overwhelm yourself.
3. Remember, you do have support networks, you're not alone in this:
    - Talk to your family, friends and teachers.
4. Stress relief:
    - Make time for yourself, do things you love.

I would like to acknowledge and thank all the people who supported me throughout my HSC especially my family, friends and teachers (you know who you are).

Shout out to my Modern History teacher Ms. Bavell who diligently marked all my essays with constructive feedback (even though there was a lot) and was always eager to help. Her passion for the subject was a true inspiration to my success.

Good luck!

BECOMING A DRAMA QUEEN

By Drew Ireland-Shead

Introduction

My name is Drew Ireland-Shead and I am a graduate from Sydney Girls High School, class of 2018.

What makes me a suitable writer of this article is my HSC results. I achieved an ATAR of 99.95 and received 2nd in the state for both Modern History and Drama. My Drama mark ended up being 99/100 and my individual performance was nominated for Onstage. My favourite part about telling people my results is the look of shock on their faces when I tell them my subjects, in particular drama. My subjects were all stereotypically considered to be "low-scaling subjects". The notion that you can't do exceedingly well in your HSC when undertaking these subjects has formed a mythological status in the minds of NSW high school students. People always consider drama as a bludge subject, a low scaling subject for people that aren't aiming high for their HSC results and just want an easy pass. I am proof that this isn't true. In fact, traditionally considered "low scaling subjects" can sometimes be easier to hack, and safer choices for success if you approach them with intelligence, which is exactly what this article aims to help you do.

Thoughts about HSC Drama

I loved drama as a subject. One of the great things about it is the freedom that it gives you. There is so much opportunity for personal experimentation and for focusing on specific aspects of theatre that you are particularly passionate about, or interested in. However, with this freedom comes quite a lot of responsibility. As a drama student, you basically have two major works, your individual project ("IP") and your group performance ("GP"). So, don't consider the subject lightly and don't ignore it for other work. So many students get carried away with the freedom and independence of the subject and don't work at it. If you take my advice and don't put off doing your work for drama, you will automatically be within the higher range of drama students. You will even be ahead of the rest of your cohort, because as a drama student, you will be finished with a good portion of your HSC examinations before the written exam period comes around. This is because the GP performances and IP presentations are finalized months before. Trust me, it feels so good to have less pressure than your friends during those four weeks of exams. Another good thing to know, a silver lining, is that the syllabus changes don't really impact drama, so all my advice is still very relevant and you can still get a lot of valuable assistance from past students, unlike those undertaking other subjects.

General advice on achieving good results

Develop, if you don't have one already, a passion for theatre.

I have loved theatre and the performing arts ever since I was young. My family have always been avid theatre goers and I was a subscriber to Sydney theatre companies from a young age. This really helped me going into drama, because I had an understanding of how theatre worked. I strongly advise you to see as many theatrical productions as you can. This doesn't have to be expensive, there are lots of cheap theatre productions everywhere. This will not only support the industry, but allow you to develop critical skills. Some productions you'll love, and some you'll hate, and from there you will learn what you believe makes a successful production. The ability to critically analyse theatre is a crucial skill that you need to develop, in order to succeed at drama. If this sounds daunting, remember the great thing about drama is that you can focus on the part of drama that you love, the aspects that made you choose the subject in the first place. Whether it's costume design, set design, acting or directing, drama is a broad discipline which allows you to write about whatever part of theatre most interests you and also complete your major work in that particular category.

The essay is the section which can set people apart.

Many drama students are natural performers, but struggle to articulate their thoughts in essay form and critically analyze theatre in a set time frame. For this reason, working on your essay writing skills can be a weapon for success. Instead of putting off developing an analysis of your set plays, start working on paragraphs and writing up practical evidence EARLY in the year. Know your plays inside and out. Truly engage with the pieces and learn to love them. Your passion will make you stand out from the crowd and I guarantee this will help you to get better overall marks than most students.

Have a unique and specific opinion.

In the exam, many students tend to fill the page with words in a way which theoretically is correct, but has no foundational argument, so their opinion gets lost. Having a specific outlook on the plays you are analyzing makes you stand out from the crowd. For example, I wrote an essay which had the following as a thesis:

Ultimately, both Stolen and Neighborhood Watch depict issues and ongoing challenges that continue to resonate with contemporary audiences, yet their use of dramatic techniques to deliberately influence the response of the audience results in an affirmation of the potential for positive outcomes for these issues.

This kind of strong and bold statement is compelling for the marker and demonstrates that you haven't just memorised a bunch of evidence, but have taken the time to think about the plays and create detailed and deep opinions on them.

Do extra research.

Don't rely on the two page handouts that everyone else in the state receives. I found a great article about how one of my plays for the "significant plays of the 21st century" topic, *Top Girls* by Caryl Churchill, can be interpreted as apt commentary on the breakdown of the concept of a successful transnational, transhistorical feminist movement in light of the capitalist framework of the late 20th century. This was a far more interesting take on the play to write about than the simple ideas that were highlighted in the HSC resources provided to me by my school intranet. So, use resources like JSTOR, your local library, google scholar or other sites. It's not plagiarism if you get inspired by what is written to develop your own ideas and opinions. Reading analysis by others helps you to see what you think is most important about the play, and also helps you articulate your ideas in a deeper and more sophisticated way.

Whatever you do,
DO NOT TREAT DRAMA LIKE ENGLISH!

English and drama are <u>very different subjects </u>and many drama markers are also trained to teach English. They therefore know the distinctions and are harsh on students that don't follow this basic yet crucial advice.

Firstly, don't accept the presumption that is sometimes promoted in English class that sophisticated language is more greatly rewarded.

Clarity is key. You don't get extra points for obscure vocabulary. Instead, concentrate on creating a flow to your argument that your marker can easily follow.

Secondly, make sure to talk about you and your experiences. Drama is not just theoretical. Like English, it is practical and experiential. This means that your markers want nothing more than for you to discuss your opinions and what you personally have experimented with in class.

Furthermore, English students are often told that the conclusions to their essays only have to be a few sentences, as they aren't a crucial part of the English essay structure. This approach is not encouraged for drama. Your conclusion in a drama essay should still be punchy and succinct, but long enough to properly rap up your argument.

As well as acknowledging the differences between drama and English, it is nonetheless important to be aware of their similarities. Drama students have an automatic advantage, as English is a compulsory subject that can supplement your drama studies way more than, for example, another student's physics class.

For one thing, context is incredibly important in both subjects. Just like English, it is important to know what was revolutionary about your studied plays when they were created and how they were shaped by their cultural environment. However, an aspect which is less discussed in English that you also need to understand for drama involves the elements of your plays which make them seminal and still important to produce. You have to ask yourself, why do directors continue to put on productions of this specific play? Books may always be available, but theatre is ephemeral, and this very quality is one to focus on in your studies.

Lessons learnt from personal experience

On the day of the exam, relax rather than over-prepare

The 2018 HSC drama exam was at midday on the very last day of the HSC timetable. This meant that I, and I'm sure many in the state-wide drama cohort, were feeling burnt out and exhausted from months of preparation, long nights at the state library and a gruelling three weeks of other exams. The night before, despite the many practice essays I had written and the hours I had spent pouring over my notes and receiving feedback from my teacher, I was so stressed that I couldn't sleep.

A friend convinced me to go to breakfast with her on the morning of the exam, instead of going over my notes yet again. This was, quite honestly, a brilliant suggestion. It is imperative to be present in the exam room in a calm and relaxed state of mind. This will absolutely not be created by cramming the day of the exam, or at least, that was not my experience. Personally, in order to write to the best of my abilities I needed, ironically, to not be in a studying headspace. I needed to rely on the months I had spent preparing and be assured that my knowledge would kick in. Focusing on being mentally calm meant that, instead of panicking and spurting out memorised sentences, I was able to form flexible arguments directly responding to the question asked of me.

This approach meant that I ended up with a 99% in that exam room.

Know your performance so well that you can perform it from muscle memory, no matter what happens

The trouble with choosing performance for your drama individual project, which most of the state wide cohort decide to do, is that you do not have the sense of security that comes with consistently drafting your portfolio, essay or costume designs, to your own assessment of perfection. No matter how much you rehearse and rehearse, you can't control what will happen on the day of your assessment.

It happened that on the day of my assessment, I was not well, mentally and physically. My trial exam period had only just come to a close and it had been incredibly rough for me, so I was by no means in the best state to be performing for my drama HSC mark. Despite being incredibly proud of my trial performance, where I was so mentally present in my characterisation that I cried whilst acting, I instead cried AFTER my HSC performance. In fact, I sobbed. I was devastated to have not performed to the best of my abilities, when it counted the most. Even my teacher admitted that my trial performance had been better.

Yet, despite being gutted at what I believed was a disappointing performance, not long after, I got called down with my classmate to our drama teacher's office to be told that our individual performances had been nominated for OnStage, a showcase of the best individual projects from around the state.

The point of this story is that your HSC markers have never seen you perform before the day they mark you. They won't feel the disappointment you will, if you don't think that you've performed your personal best that day. In order to combat the scary concept that your HSC mark rests on how you perform during eight minutes, of one random day, you need to know your piece, and your character, like the back of your hand. Although I was not as 'in the moment' as I usually was on the day of my HSC performance, I had rehearsed every detail of those eight minutes, making it so polished that even if I was a little rusty, it didn't matter. I may have felt like I was going through the motions, but the markers do not expect you to be professional actors, and even professional actors have 'off' performances. If your piece is polished, then you can rest assured that your work will be rewarded. How to polish your piece to ensure this? Look at the IP section further down this article.

My chosen individual project – Individual Performance

Make it your own

Because you can justify every directing choice you make in your logbook, you can be as creative as you want. Don't be afraid to make bold choices ; markers want you to do this. There is a saying in drama that you should always make the most unexpected or seemingly illogical decision when performing, as this will create the most interesting moments. Markers see so many performances that they are particularly engaged by those who take a unique approach to their projects. Don't stick to the same old status quo. Stay away from clichéd topics (teenage angst and the like) and hone in on a unique issue, one which resonates with you personally. You can even link things to personal experiences so as to draw out emotions within yourself and intrigue your marker in your rationale. Connecting your piece to you, and your life, in some way can elevate your performance enormously.

Beginning your piece

A really great tip which I received, and I would strongly recommend, is to start your piece with a silent moment of focus in character. Take a moment at the beginning of your piece to draw your audience in. Breathe and look out into the audience, or at a prop if you have one, as your character. Not only will this allow you to remain calm as a performer, but it will also engage your audience and marker straight away.

General direction notes

Always have moments of stillness and silence in your piece. They are moments to recapture your audience's attention and demonstrate your ability to focus. On the other hand, interesting moments of physical movement are also great weapons. They can help to showcase your performance abilities, develop your characterisation deeply and create contrast between your moments of stillness, so as to maintain the engagement of your audience.

Overall, it is important to demonstrate your range as an actor in your piece. No matter what the central atmosphere, theme, style or genre, include moments which contrast each other. For example, even if you are doing a more dramatic piece, include lighter or even funny moments, and vice versa. The various shades of grey within your piece will create depth and believability.

Monologue choices

Unless you are incredibly talented and experienced, don't choose characters that are too far away from your reality, if you are attempting to do a piece in a realism style. It is nothing against your ability to act, but it makes it harder for your maker to believe you as your character. You don't want to set yourself up for failure.

Watch videos of other people performing your monologue

You can, depending on your monologue, find examples of others' interpretations of your character on YouTube. I found watching these really helpful. Firstly, because writing my analysis of them in my logbook helped me to fill my logbook up before I handed it in to my teacher, but also because it helped me to know what I thought worked and what I thought didn't. My personal interpretation of my character was developed by taking certain elements from others and knowing which elements from others I would exclude.

Don't be afraid to change up your script

Don't forget that you are not obliged to follow your script word for word. Just like you are able to write your own script, you are allowed to scrap certain lines or write new lines into a script that has been written by a playwright. Make it perfect for you and your interpretation of your character.

Overall, experiment, take risks and don't be afraid to change it up. DONT GET STUCK in what you have created thus far. Major works are a process which involves letting things go.

The Infamous Group Performance

The group performance is, in my opinion, by far the hardest requirement of the subject. There is no point in me attempting to instruct you on how to work with your group because each group includes unique individuals, and dealing with your classmates will be a challenge which you will have to personally tackle. However, I can give you some broad tips for the play building process.

Firstly, <u>look and experiment with different styles</u>. Don't simply rely on the classic, theatresports-style comedic realism. Quite honestly, markers are sick of this. Unless you're super witty, I would suggest steering completely clear of this style. You are much more likely to intrigue your marker by employing techniques and devices from other theatrical forms and styles, and if you do these successfully, you will definitely impress your markers as well. However, in saying this, definitely be inspired by theatresports-style techniques. Moments where people in your group become inanimate objects or moments of synchronised movement can be dramatic and effective when performed well.

Secondly, <u>show off your skills</u>. Throw in moments from other things you have performed that you were really proud of. If you have talents in things like dancing or singing, include these as well. Stick to your strengths and use them to your advantage.

Thirdly, GET AS MANY PEOPLE TO WATCH IT AS POSSIBLE. This advice is also applicable to your individual performance, if you choose to do one. Getting others' opinions is critical as they can notice moments which are awkward or don't work, which you might not. A fresh pair of eyes is a great starting point if you are stuck or low on ideas. In addition, <u>consistently film your group</u> by propping up a camera in your rehearsal space. Playing back these videos helps to check that all your group members are in time and see how your ideas have visually manifested on stage.

Ultimately, the group performance is about brainstorming, playing and experimenting. As a drama student, hopefully you can appreciate the agonising process of play building, and perhaps even enjoy it. A good trick to make sure that you're still staying on track whilst experimenting is to <u>write down a couple of things that you came up with and you all particularly loved</u> at the end of every class or session with your group. Keep this list of movements, tableaux, characters or moments to insert into your piece to create something.

<u>Writing the essay</u>

The best part about drama essays is how truly easy they are to prepare for, because they are very, very predictable. Once the stress of completing the major works is over, drama rewards your hard work. There is no feeling that you are at the mercy of the devious NESA exam writers like in other subjects. If you <u>follow the syllabus and know the general ideas that your topics are about</u>, I can guarantee you will do well.

The age old question - to memorise or not to memorise

I would advise <u>against</u> memorising any essay, word for word, for any subject. However, you certainly must memorise examples in depth, perhaps full paragraphs if you can. The danger of preparing just one essay for each topic is that you have to make sure you have examples for each dramatic element, as you can be asked questions which force you to focus on specific elements. I memorised around four to six examples for each play, expanded upon in paragraph form, and then used the ones that worked best for the question on the day.

This is more work than just making a table of dramatic elements, or memorising one or two essays word for word. However, I personally found that it made me feel the most prepared and confident for any question I could receive, whilst also ensuring I had some complex sentences and well-phrased analysis already memorised.

Was learning of drama restricted to the syllabus?

You should definitely learn the syllabus off by heart. It is great to use words from the rubric in your response, to ensure that you are linking your argument to the concepts you are meant to be studying. On that note, make sure that you understand the key concepts of each topic thoroughly, not just the words. It is imperative that you read between the lines of the question given to you, to see how it connects to the syllabus and address the overarching concepts of the syllabus in every essay, no matter what the question seems to say at first glance. However, it is still important to continually reference the question throughout the essay, as for any essay in any subject.

In addition to memorising the syllabus, definitely memorise the elements of drama. If you don't already know them, when you review them they should ring a bell from your junior studies. All your evidence should connect to these elements, name drop them as often as you can.

Constructing Essays

Informality and the infamous 'I'

Drama essays are less structured and thus way less boring than English essays. Something which can at first seem uncomfortable to write when you are used to constructing essays for English is using personal pronouns. Drama requires you to write about your personal experiences and thus it is important to write from your own perspective, by using the word 'I'. Furthermore, this pronoun is the gateway to a much more informal and personal essay. Rather than the strict structure which governs the English domain, as long as your drama essay is coherent, your structure can be quite flexible. Drama markers truly want to hear YOUR opinion, so you are required to be more informal and write more passionately than in essays for other subjects. For my second HSC essay, I vividly remember writing a very ardent argument about the power of individual plays to remain relevant throughout time, due to their role in revolutionising the purpose of theatre from entertainment to social engagement. This essay was not written in a sophisticated manner, and possibly became more like a rant than anything by the conclusion. However, it was fervent and argued strongly and it captured the marker's attention. That, more than anything, will be rewarded.

In terms of structure, JUST GET TO THE POINT.

You do not have long to write your drama essays, so focus on your examples in your body paragraphs, and set up your ideas in your introduction. These examples need to clearly support your thesis, be detailed and get integrated into your argument fluidly. Essentially, the marker must never have to stop and think about what you're saying, or re-read your sentences. Be clear and make sure your marker stays with you. My teacher always liked to say that we should imagine we are holding the marker's hand, guiding them so that they don't have to work too hard to see our point. This can come in the form, for example, of re-stating elements of the question in your topic sentences, rather than saying something like 'this concept is further seen'.

Evidence

Supporting evidence to back up your thesis in a drama essay can include:

- Quotations or evidence from the text
- Evidence from relevant imagined or real productions
- Practical experiences related to the selected topic area

Remember that you don't always have to have actually done what you are discussing. You can say things like – "we discussed X concept in class", "in our theorising about the play", "in our debate surrounding the play". Furthermore, another great thing about drama essays is that, not only is stealing ideas from others accepted, it is encouraged.

For example:

> *My class was inspired by the Belvoir Street 2011 Production, which used Romani music whenever it transported the audience to Ana's past in Hungary. We explored this motif of music further, playing it as a soundscape whenever Ana discussed her refugee experiences. For example, when we workshopped the scene when Ana is told by Doctor White that she should go to a hospice, as the actor playing Ana said "All her life Ana been the prisoner, and now should to be the prisoner even in her death?" we played the music softly in the background. The motif of the song created a connection between the music and the audience, to constantly remind the audience of the large community of people that suffered the same imprisonment as Ana. Hence, the audience was influenced to associate the traumatic experiences they witnessed Ana enduring to a larger history of oppression and struggle.*

It is also important to include at least one quotation directly from the script; the markers prefer this. However, make sure the quotation serves a purpose in your argument. Sometimes I included a quotation by mentioning what I directed actors to do physically when they said a certain line, or more often, I quoted stage directions as evidence of certain theatrical choices the playwrights made.

Remember to note the acts or scenes that your evidence comes from. Although this is not required, it sets you above others, crucially demonstrating your deep understanding and knowledge of the plays you have studied.

Make sure to invent evidence.

You heard that right, this concept is literally in the syllabus.

I believe that not only is it valid, but it is perhaps more useful than any other form of evidence you can use. Creating your own evidence allows you to be creative and to write about the best things to suit your thesis and enhance your argument. You can quite permissibly create evidence out of thin air in order to prove your point. An essay writer's dream!

For example, note the invented evidence in the following paragraph:

> *However, the final scene of the play, 'Sandy at the End of the Road' positions the audience to feel positively about the potential for Indigenous Australians to reconnect with their culture. If I was to direct this scene, I would use lighting to amplify this cathartic moment, using stage lights to create a corridor of light in front of the characters. The visual of this 'road' represents the paths that allow colonial populations to possess and control territory, thus Sandy's decision to be at the 'end' of this road reflects a determination to no longer follow the path mapped out for him by white society. This lighting would allow the audience to understand that, when Sandy notes that he 'don't have to run anymore' he has recognised that he can stop being directed by others and return to his own country and the Aboriginal knowledge of 'home', rather than a Western understanding of 'home' as a stationary physical place. Furthermore, I would have the house lights come up slowly during the scene to symbolise that the audience themselves can and must be part of this process of recognition and reconciliation.*

*note: you <u>do not</u> have to say 'if'. It is perfectly acceptable to pretend that you did indeed execute whatever you are writing about, in real life.

Mention and engage with the specific theatrical style that your play is written in

This shows sophistication and enhances your analysis as it presents your evidence as an element within a larger vehicle of expression. The choice of style is incredibly important. Think about how important form is when constructing an English essay.

You can do this by writing something even as simple as, *"Neighbourhood Watch, uses non-linearity, a defining element of magic realist theatre, to create fluidity in time and space in the play, allowing for Ana's stories of struggle to teach Catherine valuable lessons for her present life,"* and then expanding on this idea in your body paragraphs with evidence of where this is seen directly in moments of the play. This will demonstrate to your marker that you understand why the playwright has chosen to write their play in a specific theatrical style, and how the techniques that fall into this style play essential roles in engaging an audience in the desired way.

Another great technique to write successful arguments is to raise the counter argument, and then disprove the counter argument ;)

This is actually a rhetorical device that I formally learnt in my history classes. However, I think that it can equally be applied to strengthen a drama essay. Here is an example where you can observe the technique.

> My class experimented with multiple casting in order to emphasise the need to recognise the Indigenous Australian experience as varied and diverse. Rather than characters, my classmates and I were given numerous vignettes, meaning that we all played multiple characters at different times. <u>Although this could be seen to negate the characters' journeys, it instead made clear the diversity and immensity of these traumatic experiences.</u> Furthermore, it depicted the experiences the characters embody as common journeys, amplifying the significance of each. Hence, the use of <u>non-naturalistic theatrical conventions</u>

(specific type of theatrical device unique to contemporary theatre) serves to influence the perspectives of an audience (central concept of theatrical analysis) of Stolen, *provoking them to understand the diversity and immensity of Indigenous Australian experiences.*

Complement your evidence with different evidence

In order to demonstrate your range as a drama student, it is imperative to show that you understand that theatre is the combination of a variety of different production elements. Don't use the same basic costuming or set choices. Including a mixture of disparate forms of evidence will reflect your awareness of how different aspects of theatrical production work in conjunction to create desired effects. In addition, it can help you to stand out from others writing about the same play.

For example, sound is a great piece of evidence to have in your arsenal, particularly when used to amplify other evidence. Sound can have a profound impact on what an audience experiences; it can form importance pieces of symbolism whilst also having a tangible role in creating the desired atmosphere and mood within the theatre. Moreover, it is so ridiculously easy to find, as it will be written directly into the stage directions.

Expanding your discussion of evidence

It is essential that you do not simply list the evidence that you are using to support your argument. Elaborating on what techniques or examples you are discussing gives them greater weight and makes your essay flow, as opposed to sounding like a rote-learnt list. A good way to expand on your evidence, if you are stuck, is to talk about how your class debriefed performances. For example, you might write about how your class discussed the experience of performing a specific scene and mention how both audience and performers within the class understood the intention and felt the effects and impacts of the techniques employed.

Overall essay advice – get inside the head of a director to focus on how your audience reacts

The relationship between actor and audience is the most important thing that you must address, no matter if the question asks for it specifically or not. Every aspect of a production is a deliberate choice which has been made to impact an audience in a specific way. Acknowledging this notion, both in your own mind and in your essay, will help you to craft strong essays. When writing, you are taking your marker into the theatre, so picture your vision in your mind, and describe it.

One way to do this is to describe the audience's reaction to a particular moment. For instance, a moment might make the audience hold their breath, sit on the edge of their chairs or empathise with a certain character.

See the following example:

> *I was an audience member for some of my classmates who workshopped the picnic scene between Catherine and Martin (Act 1, Scene 15) to emphasise Martin's role in impeding Catherine's ability to move on in her life. They did this by developing physical tension between the two characters, having Martin physically block Catherine's path across the stage. The actor playing Catherine sprinted in from stage left toward stage right but was stopped by the actor playing Martin, standing in the way, which directed the focus of the scene to Martin. The physical tension this created between the two characters highlighted that Martin's presence in Catherine's mind is blocking her from experiencing things beyond her insular world. As an audience member this poignant moment, where the two actors held focus with each other and there was a sudden stasis of movement, made me hold my breath and intensified the emotional reaction to the scene. Such a response led me to empathise with Catherine and see her struggles of isolation due to mental health as an issue faced in a modern Australian world.*

The most important thing to focus on is how the director is trying to get the audience to feel. Are they aiming to challenge them? Confront them? Force them to feel empathy or sympathy for others? Interrogating this concept is the key to writing a good drama essay.

All theatre will try and evoke strong emotional responses, but where does the play fall on the spectrum of emotion? What is its purpose? See this example:

> Furthermore, the plays <u>purposefully direct their audience to examine</u> ongoing challenges for groups within contemporary society <u>in order to stimulate positive feelings</u> surrounding the potential for reconciliation and progress within their audience.

Ultimately, remember that in your essays you are essentially answering the core dramatic question: How do theatrical elements, in conjunction, create tension and affect an audience's response to the play?

My core topic - CATP
(Contemporary Australian Theatre Practice)

In general, all the essays you will write for this topic will be about how playwrights of your studied Australian contemporary plays employ dramatic techniques and conventions to engage their audience in specific ways. As this topic is one of the core topics which every drama student across the state must study, the question will be broad. It is therefore your responsibility, in your introduction, to make your argument specific.

Personally, I tended to focus on how the playwrights of my plays, and the directors, designers and actors of particular productions, made theatrical choices to invite their audience to not only witness, but understand the issues faced by different communities in Australia.

Here is an example paragraph that I wrote:

> *Stolen* evokes an emotional resonance within its audience, contributing meaningfully through theatrical engagement to the national collective memory and challenging its audience not to slip into a morass of forgetting and ignorance. Through the interaction between the past and present in the play, the audience is positioned to see the impacts of colonisation and the legacy of the Stolen Generations not as past issues but as foundations of Aboriginal experience. In order to emphasise this notion, my class discussed producing the play on a circular, rotating set that moved as the play progresses, symbolising the progression of institutionalised racism that transcends time and society. As the actors are unable to leave the continually circulating confines of the stage, the audience would understand these characters, emblematic of wider groups of Aboriginal people, are living legacies of discrimination, racism and genocide. Furthermore, due to the episodic structure of the play, my class experimented with utilising the transitions between each vignette in a manner which would not make the audience's engagement become disjointed and instead amplify the audience's reactions. We constructed an image using drama blocks where one person pushed against the block as if trying to move it and another held the block in place on the other side. During each transition we built upon and developed this image with more blocks and actors, creating an intertextual allusion to 'The Myth of Sisyphus' designed to evoke a sense of continual oppression. This physical, poetic image highlighted the Indigenous experience as so traumatic that words can not do justice to it and further forced the audience to maintain complete immersion in the play's world. Without words they were forced to stay acutely aware of what is happening on the stage. Hence, *Stolen* encourages its audience to recognise that the discrimination Indigenous people have faced as a social group continues to impact on their lives and continues to make them feel like 'outsiders' in the population.

One of the beauties of theatre is how it makes certain experiences of groups within our society accessible to a wider audience. This is a facet which you should focus on, as historically many essay questions have mentioned this notion. If you understand this concept, then it follows that there were social and cultural concerns pertinent to the time when the playwrights wrote, which instigated their desire to reveal aspects of certain Australian experiences. Yet theatre makers often face the task of ensuring that the productions of these plays still remain relevant to today's society. A unique and interesting thing to include in your essay could be a production element which connects the themes of your plays to a contemporary concern, a way which grounds the cultural ideas being explored, in the present, for an audience. This would definitely be received well by a marker.

Don't ignore the CONTEMPORARY in the title of the topic

Know what it means when a play is contemporary theatre. This description does not just refer to when the play was written. There are theatrical choices that are unique to this label, techniques and devices which you can highlight as contemporary as to link to the overarching concepts of the syllabus. Make sure to memorise techniques which are specifically contemporary, including those such as:

- Multimedia devices
- Non-linear structures
- Symbolic physical images on stage, rather than realistic physical settings and movements
- Techniques which engage all the senses, e.g. smells in the theatre which create immersive experiences

Furthermore, think about and articulate why it is that these techniques have become central to contemporary theatre. What do they help the playwright and director to communicate? Why are they chosen over techniques from other types of theatre?

For example, consider how a technique "exemplifies the contemporary rejection of the conventional escapist experience of the theatre", or how contemporary devices and non-linear structures allow playwrights and directors to present issues in a more multi-dimensional and powerful manner than realism or naturalism allows.

My Elective Topic - Significant Plays of the 20th Century

The twentieth century was a period of social, technological and global cultural change like no other. The world was devastated by not one, but two world wars; major advances in technology created new ways of communicating and living; and long held structures and beliefs in societies began to shift. As always, theatre held up a mirror to the world, reflecting the changes and events around it.

This unit was by far my favourite part of the drama syllabus because the plays were so incredibly interesting and exciting to both perform and watch, due to the theatrical experimentation that characterizes the plays.

The most essential part to focus on when discussing this topic is how the works "<u>shifted and influenced the theatrical paradigm of the 20th century</u>", to quote the first sentence of the syllabus paragraph. In general, try and focus on how:

- both plays were relevant to their specific contexts, yet applicable to the universal;

- both plays redefined the purpose of theatre and drama, not just as a reflection of human life, but also a piece of social commentary that criticises and discusses relevant matters and social issues (politics being only one);

- both plays aimed to test the limits and vitality of traditional and orthodox bourgeois theatre; and

- both plays formed an important part of the theatrical landscape for many years to come.

In this topic, <u>the syllabus is your best friend</u> because it essentially lists every aspect of these plays that you can be asked about and you can discuss. If you directly use the language from the syllabus, that is a great start. Focus on the following key features of the syllabus and make sure you understand them in detail:

- <u>revolutionary</u> in response to the place and time of the original production (context);

- <u>challenging</u> content, reinvented or created new theatrical styles, structures and forms (it is crucial that you understand the form and style that your plays are written in for this topic);

- the <u>impact</u> of the performance and narrative styles, issues, techniques, conventions, staging of the plays; and

- how they <u>broke new ground</u> and sought to <u>affect an audience</u> in <u>dynamic and powerful</u> ways.

At the most essential level, all theatre aims to affect an audience in a particular way and so all your essays should be based on the different ways that the plays you have studied have done that. For this topic it is imperative that you focus on how the plays you have studied aimed to change how theatre impacted its audience, and the methods they used to make this change. Caryl Churchill once stated, "playwrights don't give answers; they ask questions". I believe this quote is a beautiful summary of how the significant plays prescribed in this topic embody the notion of theatre as a springboard for social change. The discussion and exploration of ideas in the artistic sphere engages an audience and prompts them to engage in the world around them.

As always, have a specific and unique take on each play, rather than sticking to a basic analysis. See my group's focus on Churchill's exploration of the inter-sexual debate within the feminist movement, outlined below:

We have decided to focus on the changing idea of 'sisterhood' in response to Caryl Churchill's context, when Capitalism and Thatcherism fostered a new wave of feminist theatre that challenged and revolutionised earlier representations of women, and women's relationships, in theatre.

Our performance seeks to breakdown the idealised notion of transnational, trans-historical sisterhood, an ideal proclaimed by the first feminist movement in the early 20th century, due to the absence of a shared cultural framework and the lack of unity in the female experience.

Preparing for the exam

How my class prepared for this topic, and how I suggest you do too, is by making a table -- a classic.

In the table we included basic phrases and dot points but also theoretical and experiential examples. Reviewing this table before an exam allowed me to respond to any question that could be formed. Our table was similar to the following structure:

ASPECT OF RUBIC	PLAY 1	PLAY 2
Context		
Costuming		
Characterisation		
Narrative styles		
Issues (MOVE TOWARD THEATRE AS FORM OF SOCIAL CRITIQUE AND COMMENT)		
Conventions (the challenging of traditional and the reinvention of new)		

Narrative structure		
Theatrical style (e.g. the movement away from realism toward surrealism or absurdism)		
Forms (e.g. socialist theatre)		
Staging		
Actor-audience relationship		
Other new techniques (e.g. the move from Stanifslaski representational acting to Brechtian presentational acting) can include dramatic elements such as: • movement • language • sound		
Revolutionary status		

For all of the subheadings within this table, the notes that you write for each play can be used as evidence for *how the plays shifted the theatrical paradigm*, the central concept that you will be discussing in your essay. I also utilised the following table for each play individually, constructed after workshopping them in class:

ELEMENTS WHICH MAKE SIGNIFICANT PLAYS OF THE 20th CENTURY REVOLUTIONARY:	HOW THE PLAY REVOLUTIONISED THEATRE:	HOW WE EMOHASISED THIS IN OUR DEVISED PERFORMANCE:
REVOLUTIONARY TO THE PALCE AND TIME OF THE ORIGIONAL PRODUCTION	• Discussion of 'taboo' subject matter • Use of innovative techniques, which CHANGED the theatrical styles and devices which have continued to be used.	

CHALLENGING CONTENT	Broke down the idealistic notion of 'sisterhood' by emphasising the difference between individual achievement in a capitalist society and social change.	We have chosen to indicate the difference between social change and individual achievement through the contrasting distances between the actors and characters in the two scenes and through the costuming and the use of 'cross-dressing,' which at first seems to unite the characters, but only covers up underlying differences.
REINVENTED/ CREATED NEW THEATRICAL STYLES STRUCTURES AND FORMS	Top Girls is a subtle underplay working with archetypes and conventions of the time – it mixtures scenes focused on a more realistic style with stylistic scenes resonant of the changing artistic movements at the time. Top Girls also had an ambiguous ending.	We chose to much together the stylistic, dream-like first scene with the more legalistic style of the final scene – demonstrating the unity of the women as a fantasy which contracts greatly against the reality of disconnection
ENGAGE WITH 1. NARRATIVE STYPES 2. ISSUES 3. TECHNIQUES 4. STAGING OF THE PLAY	Overlapping dialogue: Non-linearity: Mixture of characters from different times: Double casting: All women cast: Historical reference: Harriette M. Morelli (in her graduate thesis: Churchill resists taking sisterhood for granted; highlighted in our piece. For example, with Joyce's dismissal of Marlene's claim "but we are friends anyway." Her play recognises that any hope for female solidarity lies in acknowledging and	Overlapping dialogue: We focused on Churchill's use of overlapping dialogue to emphasise the disconnection between the female characters. Non-linearity: We have also employed non-linearity, as similarly to Churchill's production, our scenes flow on from each other in a seemingly incongruent way. However, these scenes are juxtaposed as they both contrast to and complement each other, allowing us to explore different social spheres where women are not united (the work and domestic spheres) and contrast

overcoming not suppressing, the differences between women.

"Churchill utilises alienation effects to narrate her class and gender sorry, to instruct her audience about the need for social change… She… presents history as comedy in an attempt to infuse her audience with an awareness about the futility of individual emancipation without concurrent social transformation"

The Women "represent decidedly different social classes and they experience profoundly different existential realities.

As Bertolt Brecht suggests in his "A Shot Organum for the Threat" (1949), the representation on stage of such differences helps epic dramatists foster a critical attitude in their audience:

"If we ensure that our characters on the stage are moved by social impulses and that these differ according to the period, then we make it harder for our spectator to identify himself with them, he cannot simply feel: that's how I would act, but at most can say: If I had lived under those circumstances, and if we play works dealing with our own time as though they were historical, then perhaps the circumstances under which he himself acts with a surface-level idea and the reality of the idea, as manifested in a capitalist world.

Double casting/mixture of characters:

We choose to combine the characters in the dinner scene, which we think develops the characters as more complex.

This furthers the idea reinforced by Churchill's original double-casting (which we have also employed), which suggests the complexities of female experiences and the inability for women to be labelled or condoned into one specific "role" in society.

All women cast:

The dissonance between the characters, emphasised by the overlapping-dialogue, develops the idea that WOMEN are competing with each other, and allowing the oppression of other women to occur.

Historical reference:

Likewise, we have tried to incorporate lots of comedic moments into the first scene, including the story of Jona giving birth on the street, and some more comedic arguments between the women.

In addition, the presentation of women, clearly from other times, in a contemporary situation, highlights how audiences should continue to question their contemporary society as well as historical.

	strike his as equally odd: and this is where the critical attitude begins."	
	By setting these women together in a contemporary situation, Churchill thus constructs the present as just one of history's time periods.	

Exam techniques

Think about what direction the question wants you to take your essay in, ask yourself which specific bit from the syllabus it is focused on, and hone in on that aspect. This demonstrates that you can recognise the basis of the subject through the veil of exam questions. In addition, make sure to engage with every aspect of the question. Take the time to underline the key words and never overlook a single word used in the question; they are ALL chosen very carefully. Many students tend to see one word that they recognise and can work with and proceed to ignore the rest of the words of the question in their response, often pumping out prepared essays. This is very easily seen by markers. They are looking for how you connect the various ideas and words in the question together cohesively. Furthermore, make sure to use the words of the question constantly throughout your essay. This is one way to ensure that, no matter how much you really did memorise word for word and then copy out in the exam room, the marker can't mark you down for *not answering the question.*

Things I would have done differently

Studying smarter, not harder

How bittersweet this truism sounds. We all hear it at the beginning of our HSC journey, yet many of us choose to ignore it.

I heard this advice profusely from older students when I began my HSC and I am ashamed to admit, as I am passing it down, that I definitely did not follow it as closely as I should have. This is honestly the number one trick for acing your HSC. Figuring out what you actually need to do to achieve your desired result, rather than doing way more than is necessary.

Instead of sitting in a library for hours on end highlighting booklet upon booklet of the same analysis or the same exemplar practice essays, only half of which you are probably processing in your mind, practise articulating your thoughts! Obviously, the best way to do this is to write practice responses; but if you are the type of person which absolutely detests such a thing, and I knew plenty of people that vehemently felt this way, then force your friends, family or teachers to engage in regular discussions with you. Getting people to quiz you and practising breaking down questions with arguments and evidence is the most effective study technique to give you the maximum results, with the least amount of effort.

This way, you are more relaxed, less stressed, able to participate in other things besides studying, avoid that dreaded HSC burnout and cross that less than perfect finishing line .

Experimenting with my GP more from the beginning

There is a temptation to just go with the first idea that all the members of your group agree on, because even this is tricky enough, and time can be felt like slipping away. But trust me when I say that if you don't love what you have, leave it and move on. My group pulled apart our GP completely after trials and re-worked the whole piece in a few weeks before our HSC exam, and I am truly glad we did, because the final product was so much better than what we originally had. My principal suggested to our group that we experiment with our chosen theatrical style, and after following this advice and choosing to direct our piece in a surrealist rather than realist style, we realised the value of reaching outside our comfort zones. I would advise every drama student to experiment as much as possible, and as early as possible, and never settle on a concept which can be improved upon.

Final Advice

Don't be afraid to ask for help. I was always that kid in class that annoyed every other student because I asked so many questions. I did not hold back asking questions if I needed something to be clarified or expanded upon. Don't feel self-conscious or embarrassed to speak up in class, because sometimes making a fool of myself because I didn't know something meant that I came to understand it better. I strongly believe that this constant questioning and clarifying was crucial to my receiving a 99.95 ATAR and two State Ranks. So, hand-in as many practice tasks to your teachers as possible, use all the resources provided to you and ask for extra guidance from your mentors within your school. I know that some people are more reserved in class, so don't feel like you have to raise your voice there. You will find that teachers have a special place in their hearts, and their busy schedules, to help Year 12 students. Ask to speak to your teachers privately and I am sure they will be absolutely happy to answer your queries and assist you with your work. On that note, don't be afraid to make mistakes and don't avoid handing in work to your teachers because you are afraid of them pulling you up for these mistakes. Every critique and comment you get now is one less that your HSC marker will make when it counts. Pride will be your greatest downfall.

Finally, and of paramount importance, support your classmates. It is undoubtedly true that the better your classmates do, the better you do. I will always be indebted to my classmate, an extraordinarily intelligent student, who came first in the state in modern history. Because of her amazing achievement, and because I was behind her in our internal ranks, I was able to claim second. That fact is a reminder of the importance of sharing notes, instigating and participating in class discussions and looking out for the mental well-being of your peers. Not only will scaling help you academically, but working together with your year group will foster a positive and uplifting environment in which everyone can achieve their best.

Good luck and break a leg!

SUCCESS WITH ECONOMICS

By John Bivell

"Valar dohaeris" – High Valyrian Proverb

Hello! My name is John Bivell. I went to Fort Street High School in the Class of 2018. I topped NSW in the 2017 Earth and Environmental Science HSC in Year 11 and topped Economics in the 2018 HSC, with an ATAR of 99.90 and a mark of 98 in both subjects.

People often talk of "surviving" the HSC, and that's really not the way to think about it. The most you can say is that you have to complete a series of complex tasks. The reason the HSC appears hard is the pressure placed upon us, mostly internalised pressure from parents, reinforced occasionally (if you go to a strict school) by teachers. So, the number one way to mentally "survive" the HSC – and indeed any extended project – is that simple yet incredibly courageous skill of asking others to give you space.

In this regard, I was lucky – my parents encouraged me to take my own path, as long as it's ethical and I get the job done. And my school placed a lot of emphasis on doing things ourselves, our own way. So in terms of learning with independence, I was very privileged, and I know many people wanting to do well do not have that freedom. On the other hand, I've had friends who get fairly average results but do so stress-free, *because they knew what they wanted and the HSC was only part of it.* Discovering what kind of creature you are isn't revolutionary, just part of growing up. Your challenge is doing it while juggling an antiquated education system as well as your parents' best wishes and worst fears about your future.

But of course, *valar dohaeris*. Good luck!!!

1. General HSC Tips

<u>Sleep</u>

Make sure you sleep 7-9 hours. The dux of my school slept at 10 and woke at 6. You know people who study little because they just *get* things? It's because they sleep and their brain is switched on.

<u>Social media management</u>

If you need more time, you've gotta control your phone hours. You'll have the rest of your life to message friends, and no-one's Insta story is more interesting than your own lived experience. At the end of the day, it's up to you.

If you manage social media with apps/Chrome extensions like StayFocused or Forest, then you can make time for proper relationships as well as free up study time. You can try willpower, but it's unlikely to work. So deleting apps during exam periods is definitely worthwhile.

<u>Time management</u> – see comments above. Everything else is secondary.

Regarding how much time should be spent studying, an hour a day is more than enough. I personally did about two hours every 2-3 days as my term-time study pattern, but in hindsight, it would have been better to spread it out. What work should you do? Remember that teachers must teach to the class average, not to you. In reality, one subject might take you two days to understand while another takes two minutes – *but teachers give homework equally*. Therefore, **prioritise** your worst subjects.

Sit down with a piece of paper and think: what activity in the most objective sense will boost my marks the most? That requires a lot of thinking about where you're going and where your marks are headed, which means you actually understand how you, as a HSC entity, function.

Enjoy the process

The key with the HSC, weirdly enough, is to not be too fussed about the result. That way, you focus exclusively on **enjoying the process** (so choose enjoyable, interesting or challenging engaging) subjects), eliminating stress and gaining motivation.

Motivation

If you focus on the process, then you end up, say, writing an essay or doing a past paper with the express objective of *writing an essay or doing a past paper*, rather than trying to second guess the system as well as your own ability.

So there you have it - High School in a nutshell. Oh, and with Years 7-10, have as much fun as possible, play sports, learn music, have hobbies, and be young! Sit apart from your friends and listen in your worst class (probably maths or English) and do any work that's required so you don't cripple yourself for senior school. Everything else? Take it easy. Even in Year 11 aim for the minimum, then ramp it up in Year 12. This was advice given to me by every graduating Year 12 and it's advice I'm giving to you now.

2. Tips on Studying Economics

Most subjects in the HSC are largely quite ordinary with a dash of fascinating. Not so with Economics. It is probably the most "legit" subject in the HSC apart from maths, and while it is the hardest social science, it is one of, if not the, most rewarding.

Why? This is because it deals with the real world and forces you to be up-to-date with it. The theory is also incredibly interesting once you get the hang of it, and it provides a really good model for understanding the world and society around you. A few years ago, NESA deleted Extension Economics (which included cool things like Marxism and environmental critiques of capitalism) and squished the content into the 2-unit course, which means there is a mother lode of content. A memory game, to be sure, but a welcome one.

At its core, Economics is about understanding why people do things with their lives. It is quite reductive because it reduces people to models and statistics. If you accept that the human is both an animal and a Hamlet-esque 'in-apprehension-how-like-a-god' Enlightenment sage, then Economics assumes we are the former. Fun!

How to study for Economics

In the week of holidays before term resumes, read the textbook chapters **ahead** of time that you will be covering and make notes. You'll feel more confident when the teacher teaches and you already know it, and confidence is half the HSC game anyway. Plus it means you can go beyond the basics, such as reading *The Economist, ABC, SBS, Sydney Morning Herald, Australian Financial Review* (the best in my opinion, I take it in paper form) and any other overseas publications like *The New York Times*. Also, RBA speeches and publications or ABS posts. Then when exam time rolls around, ramp up the revision and you can get to doing past papers ASAP.

How to take notes

I get the textbook and other materials, read them, figure out what's going on and make my notes really creative! With diagrams, lists, little bubbles of text everywhere (all on blank paper), just make it all fit on one page and don't write full sentences (or even dot points if you can avoid it, just words or phrases). Include graphs everywhere.

After Trials, when I seriously doubted my Economics ability, I shifted from the above method to reading the textbook (*Australia in the Global Economy* by Tim Dixon and John O'Mahoney, and you <u>must</u> get the most recent edition) from cover to cover, **highlighting like crazy** anything and everything. I also wrote notes in the margins, summarising fat paragraphs into dot points of one word or phrase, etc. Also condensing paragraphs with lots of random statistics into tables for comparison and memorisation, plus including things I found in other textbooks or online. I then did the accompanying workbook exam after each chapter. If that sounds like a trek, I compressed this work all into one week about five weeks after Trials ended (so starting to study again). I marked my answers; but beware, the online Pearson answers are sometimes incorrect, so cross-reference with a friend or Economics class Facebook page if you're keen.

3. What are the components of Economics?

<u>Multiple Choice</u>

You should be able eventually to 20/20 this section on most papers unless its 2016 or 2018. It's mostly common sense and memory, i.e. read every single thing in the textbook at least once, because those last few questions will try and get you with some minor fact or distinction. The 2018 HSC MC was all obscure labour markets facts that you can't go by common sense, so I trusted my gut and went with the option that seemed to resonate the most with the voices in my subconscious. Other than that, do your calculations thrice, read the question, stay focused and you won't make silly mistakes. Cross out answers in a process of elimination.

When I was studying for the final HSC exams, if I didn't want to do anything strenuous, I would just do a past paper MC, nice and easy guessing game. I practised speed to get 11 minutes consistently, but harder papers took to 15 (my actual HSC was 29).

Short Answer

Write as fast as possible! Spend 5-10 seconds planning out an answer. Spam detail, write neatly but quickly. Go beyond the lines. If you do the whole Dixon workbook then you've covered basically everything, except if they toss in a curved ball, in which case don't panic, answer it. I didn't do any past paper short answer questions, but in the five days before HSC I read over every short answer question, marking guideline and sample answer. It takes 15 minutes per HSC paper, you'll finish them all in no time. If it's an internal school exam then appeal your marks. Clear expression is important. Use short sentences. Give sample answers to a friend and see if they can understand your handwriting and sentences. Aim to full mark it.

Essays

Ahh, the bane of my HSC existence! These are so hard to nail, 45-55 minutes each in the exam. **Don't** use running writing. Practise printing at speed, 20-30 words per minute. Write a minimum of 800 words. Messy handwriting lost me so many marks over the HSC. If it's clean and neat they will throw marks at you.

This is how I approached essays:

1. Get a copy of Spencer and George's essay plans in PDF.. It's one of the most popular study aids full of good material. It teaches the basics of structure and style.

2. Get a hold of a Google drive full of state ranking essays. My school cohort had one passed down from state rankers in 2011 and 2014. If you don't have one, ask a friend to share the link for their school drive. Otherwise, get essays online or from teachers.

3. Read a state ranking essay in depth, making a detailed mind map of the whole essay. Include outside graphs and stats. It should take 30-40 minutes.

4. Close the essay and (hand) write an essay from the mind map only, no running writing. Use their structure. Mimic their style! Especially repeat their catchphrases or recurring descriptors used in intros and conclusions, e.g. "macroeconomic policy *mix*" or "limitations of economic policy" or "2-3% on average over the course of the economic cycle." You'll notice the best essay paragraphs *integrate theory with contemporary understanding* (best advice my teacher ever gave me). Here is an example paragraph evaluating environmental policy:

> *Another policy used to achieve environmental sustainability in Australia was the 2011 carbon tax (Year 6 simplicity) to reduce climate change. The carbon tax was a market based policy that incorporated the social cost of the negative externality of greenhouse gas pollution into the market price or private cost of electricity (syllabus, tick) by pricing carbon at (something) dollars per tonne (contemporary understanding integrated), known as internalising the externality. This price increase from $P_{EQUILIBRIUM}$ to $P_{SOCIAL\ OPTIMUM}$ in Figure 1 (you have a negative externality diagram that you constantly refer to) causes supply to shift from $S_{EQUILIBRIUM}$ to $S_{SOCIAL\ OPTIMUM}$, reducing the quantity of the demerit good produced from $Q_{EQUILIBRIUM}$ to $Q_{SOCIAL\ OPTIMUM}$. This lead to a (something) per cent reduction in greenhouse gas emissions from the electricity sector between (year) and (year) (contemporary understanding), reducing pollution and increasing environmental sustainability as a successful environmental policy (evaluation). However, the policy also led to a deadweight loss, (syllabus theory) shaded, of (something) dollars (the economic cost, or perhaps electricity price rise) in (year), harming the economy by increasing electricity prices and factor inputs. This reduces aggregate supply from AS_1 to AS_2 in Figure 2 (an AD/AS diagram). This exemplifies a limitation of market based environmental policies regarding a short term trade off with economic growth, reducing real output from Q_1 to Q_2. Similarly, a short term election cycle also limits the viability of this environmental policy given its short term harms to households, exemplified by the carbon tax repeal in 2013 by the Abbott Government's election.*

> *Therefore, while the carbon tax was effective as a policy at achieving environmental sustainability to reduce climate change, its limitations make it less successful than (depends on your essay thesis…say,) regulation.*

5. Congratulations - the mind-map method means you just practised how to write in the style of an Economics essay, learned a pre-prepared essay for a syllabus area, as well as absorbed new stats. The best way to memorise content is to put it in essays. If you really want to do well then do this once a week. Personally I did this in the month leading up to Paper 1.

6. Learn all the graphs to include: market diagrams, AD/AS diagrams, income-expenditure diagrams, merit/demerit good diagrams, tariff/subsidy/quota diagrams, exchange rate diagrams, market floors/ceilings (for labour markets), J-curve for dollar depreciations, Kuznet's curve, LAFER curve, LRAC for economies of scale, business cycle graph, marginal efficiency of capital diagram, cash rate diagram for overnight money market (the one with perfectly inelastic supply).

4. Other Thoughts

Presentation/PowerPoint assignment

Explain everything in the shortest way possible, so you can overwhelm them with information and stats. You want the markers not to be lost, but rather be so impressed that they believe they ought to have known the content you're showing them. Also, have a metric/judgement slide you keep returning to that slowly fills up with your evaluation.

Stat pack

This is very important! Basically it's a huge compilation of raw data on all areas of Economics, that includes statistics, case studies, tables, programs, policies, etc. I grabbed mine from the internal 1st in

Economics from the year above me at my school, read it all once, and had it open when writing essays so I wasn't lost for stats. (The best way to memorise is to use in essays, remember?) Again, ask around if you don't want to make your own.

Other recommended materials

I have already mentioned *Australia in the Global Economy* (textbook and workbook), Google drive, Spencer and George essay plans (reading), and stat pack. Other material I used included 2017 1st in NSW Economics notes (bought from the Internet for $10, mostly a textbook summary), and Riley textbook (for China case study).

Tutoring

I never tried tutoring myself, but it is good for those needing motivation or learning help, with parents who can afford it.

To Conclude

In conclusion, have a very merry Year 12! Despite the lows, Year 12 also has the greatest highs, and afterwards you'll only remember the best parts. Don't take the HSC (or anything really) too seriously, and you'll do just fine. As my old principal (bless her soul) used to say… "Stay safe, have fun!"

BE A TOP ACHIEVER IN GEOGRAPHY AND CHEMISTRY

By Eleanor Lawton-Wade

> *"Don't climb a mountain so that people can see you. Climb the mountain so that you can see the world"* – David McCullough Jr

Introduction

Hello! My name is Eleanor Lawton-Wade, and I completed Year 12 in 2018 as a member of PLC Sydney. I was fortunate enough to be awarded Dux of Year 12 and to obtain an ATAR of 99.95 whilst having the privilege of serving as school vice-captain throughout my final year. For as long as I can remember I have been passionate about the world and finding out about it. Alongside academic pursuits, I have an avid interest in debating and public speaking. I spent three years on the national debating and public speaking team and have been honoured to be crowned both Australian and World champion.

Having completed high school, I am commencing a university degree in medicine. My ambitions within this career are to combine ground breaking science with compassion and kindness whilst finding a way to ensure that advances in healthcare are not only limited to people and parts of the world that have the economic capital to access them I hope to one day combine a love for science with my drive to serve people in a way that leaves the world I leave a little bit better than the one I inherited.. I am the product of family and friends who have shown infinite amount of love, patience and understanding towards me; I aim to make them proud of who I am and what I do with my abilities. Finally, I strive to live a life where not a day goes by where I don't know what it is to love and to be loved.

High school in a nutshell

I see all the opportunities that the world can offer you as a series of doors. High school is the place where you learn which key you want to use and how to use it. Hence, it is a fantastic opportunity to learn what sort of person you want to become whilst hopefully acquiring a lifelong love of learning. High school, like life in general, has equal ups and downs. Yet, it is the ups that forge memories that last a lifetime and the downs that forge resilience, kindness and perseverance in a human being. Having completed the high school journey, I say, and I honestly mean this, that you should savour every minute of your high school experience.

General advice on surviving the HSC.

<u>Know why you are</u>

Understanding who you are as a person is far more important than getting high marks. According to the commissioner for children and young people, 1 in 10 of adolescent suicides in NSW has been attributed to the pressure to perform well in the HSC. To me, that figure is sickening. Throughout the next 12 months it is crucial that you maintain your personhood by surrounding yourself with loved ones and doing things you like other than studying, so that when the emphasis shifts away from marks and ATARs you haven't lost your true identity.

Enjoy the Experience

Enjoy the experience. As cheesy as it might sound, your HSC year is filled with some extraordinary memories and experiences. Savour the good times and allow yourself to have fun, because it is those elements of Year 12 that will keep you going when times are tough.

Hold on to the opportunities

Remember how lucky you are. It is easy to become fixated on the hardships of exams, assessments and marks and forget that an education in Australia, and by extension the HSC, is an opportunity that so many around the world do not get. Therefore, rather than being overwhelmed by the magnitude of work, perceive it as an opportunity to acquire knowledge that so many will never have.

Keep yourself busy

Throughout year 12 I remained a member of two bands, played sport, continued my commitment with internal school clubs, served on the SRC and acted as school vice captain. In addition, I competed on the National Debating and Public Speaking Team and travelled to Cape Town in my HSC year. I found having a lot to do enhanced my studies because it improved my productivity in the time I did have and provided a great opportunity to relax and "switch off" for a little bit.

Manage time well

In year 12 it is easy to spend too much time on a single task, rather than spreading yourself evenly between your 10-12 units. Therefore, I would allocate a time that I was comfortable spending on a task before I commenced it and work to a timer. If I didn't complete the task in the allotted time, I would consider very carefully whether continuing the task would be of great benefit or whether there was a more productive use of my time. Therefore, in school term my study timetable would look like this:

MONDAY	PRIORITY	TASK	PLANNED TIME	ACTUAL TIME	Flow on things than need to be done in response.
	1	Complete chemistry homework due tomorrow.	40 minutes	40 minutes	Ask my teacher a question read diagrams showing structure and bonding.
	1	Complete practice English paper 2 under timed condition and review	2 hours 15 minutes	2 hours 30 minutes	Revise contextual outline for modules and dramatic techniques.
	2	Physics syllabus dot point notes	1 hour	1 hour	Finalise the skills outcome notes.

Prioritising tasks in terms of both their urgency and how beneficial their completion would be allows you to ensure that you achieve maximum output for the time you spend studying. During the holidays, my study timetable was very similar, but with a few key changes:

1. I allocated study breaks every 2-3 hours. Breaks do not include continuing to sit at your desk on social media but should actually include changing your environment, going for a walk or eating a balanced meal.

2. My HSC timetable was very spread out. Therefore, I would timetable entire days where I would not complete any study. These days were crucial for cementing my long-term memory of subjects and allowing time for my brain and body to completely relax.

There will be times in the HSC that are stressful; to imagine otherwise is to underestimate the amount of work you need for high attainment. However, there is a fine line between the pressure that constantly reminds you that the next 12 months are important and a level of stress that is harmful and counterproductive. Having the insight to know when you have crossed that line is one of the best skills to have in the HSC and in life in general. Personally, I found maintaining diversity in my HSC life, through debating, public speaking, music and sport, prevented the stress associated with fixation on a single goal. In terms of motivation, I pushed myself to achieve success because, for me, it was the best way to say thank you to my parents and teachers for everything that they had ever done for me. Further, education like the one I received is a gift, and certainly not something that should ever be taken for granted. Therefore, I felt compelled to make the most of the opportunities given to me, which was my way of expression gratitude that I was fortunate enough to be born in this country at this time.

GEOGRAPHY

<u>The importance of the syllabus.</u>

Geography is a syllabus-based subject. Therefore, a strong understanding of the syllabus requirements, including definitions, directive terms and case studies, is of the upmost importance. This is a particularly important point as many of the questions in the short answer section are directly derived from syllabus terminology. Consequently, I advise structuring geography notes accordingly:

1	Syllabus wording
2	Key definitions
3	Explanation of the ideas related to the dot point
4	Key facts, statistics and case studies that illustrate the ideas
5	Diagrams and maps that could be used in an essay related to this syllabus point.

Case Studies

Strong, diverse and reliable case studies are what distinguish excellent geography candidates from good ones. There are a limited number of HSC Geography textbooks available, which means that only providing case studies and statistics from the textbook-although it does show a level of understanding, is unlikely to impress the marker. The notes from the marking centre consistently reveal that the top marks go to students who can impress the marker with the diversity of their knowledge. Therefore, here is my advice for case studies and illustrative examples:

Often, it is better to **know many smaller examples** than compose an entire essay based on one illustrative example, even if you have strong information on it. The exception to this rule is essays that ask you to write about one economic enterprise of your choice, in which case in depth study is required. However, an essay that is able to talk about tourism in Australia, Syria and the Caribbean evidences a greater scope of understanding than an essay that focuses solely on tourism in Dubai.

Use a **diverse range of sources**, including reliable sources not specifically designed for HSC Geography candidates. For example, here are some great sources that are not commonly used in essays but contain fantastic information:

Source	What to use it for
The Intergovernmental Panel on Climate Change.	1. Ecosystems at risk; climate change is an example of a factor leading to ecosystem vulnerability. Likewise, adaptations in organisms are commonly catalysed by climatic change. 2. Tourism; climate change is a strong example of a biophysical factor that affects the nature of tourism. For instance, intensifying storm cells and wave surges associated with climatic change increase the future vulnerability of coastal regions.

	3.	Megacities; displacement caused by changing weather patterns associated with climate change can account for large rural to urban migration.
State tourism websites e.g. Tourism Queensland	1.	Economic activity; tourism.
QANTAS centre for travel and tourism economics	1.	Economic activity; tourism. Data from this source allows you to show how a range of factors influences flight paths and key travel destinations within Australia.
	2.	Economic enterprise; observing the location of flight paths and regional airports makes for a strong discussion on how locational factors influences the nature and character of an Australian economic enterprise.
Great Barrier Reef Marine Park Authority Sources	1.	Ecosystems at Risk
	2.	Economic activity; biophysical factors that influence tourism.
NGO pilot programs	1.	Research into pioneering pilot programs within megacities distinguishes essays addressing the challenges of living in megacities. For instance, the Orangi Pilot Program in Karachi Pakistan.

3. Use case studies in the **short answer section.** Often candidates believe that examples and case studies are only required in the essay section, and that the short answer section only tests theory. This, however, is not the case. Using clear and concise illustrative examples in the short answer section is often the difference between a 4 or 5 out of 6-mark question and a full mark response. This is why learning the skill of **integrating brief facts** is highly important.

Let's see an example answer to a question in *Geography paper*. Integration of illustrative example is highlighted in **bold**.

> *Outline ONE challenge of living in a megacity in the developing world (3 marks)*

Response:

> One challenge of living in a megacity is the provision of shelter. This challenge arises when population growth and housing demand exceeds supply so inhabitants are forced into already squalid areas. Added to the problem is the threat of eviction due to urban beautification and government policy. **One third of the worlds urban population lives in slums or squatter settlements, a figure that evidences the scale of the problem.**

Excelling at the essay section

Writing a geography essay can appear like a daunting task because it requires different skills than writing an English essay. However, there are a few simple tricks and essay templates that I utilised that allowed me to produce strong, well-structured responses regardless of the essay question.

An ideal structure and elements of a geography essay response should have:

An introduction that includes

1. a general overview of the nature of the enterprise, activity or ecosystem that the response addresses. The description of the nature should include the following:
   - name
   - location, including latitude and longitude and a labelled map
   - size
   - general description, including a few key statistics
2. what the essay seeks to explain/describe/evaluate. In general, this should be your unique response to the premise of the question.

Outline the points that will be used to prove your argument. The points outlined in this section should become the subheadings in the body of your essay.

Body paragraph(s)

The title of the body paragraph should be underlined. This title should be brief and give a general overview of the material addressed within. For instance, if you were to respond to the following question:

> *Describe the factors that affect the nature, spatial patterns and future directions of an economic activity in a global context.*

Your first underlined title may be:

Factor one: Biophysical.

You should provide an overview of the issue being addressed in the paragraph and how it answers the requirements of the question.

You should back up your point by numerous case study examples and relevant and reliable facts and statistics. Additionally, strong essay responses commonly include maps or diagrams within the body paragraphs to further the point.

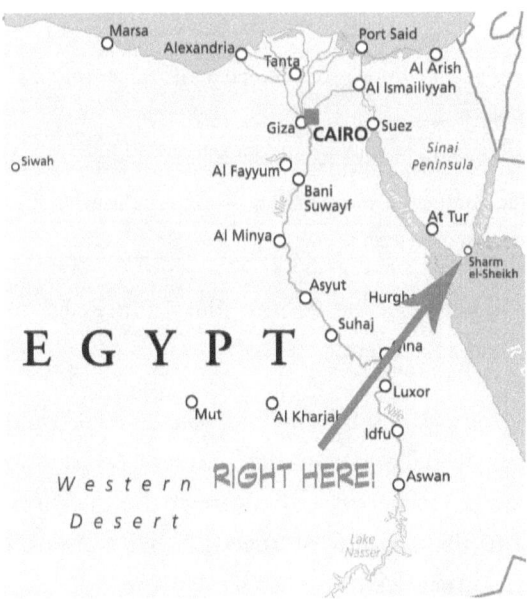

For instance, in an essay explaining how political factors moderate the spatial distribution of tourism, a map showing Sharm el Shiekh's location within the Middle East can be used to show how a volatile political climate leads to spatial exclusion of the economic activity.

(Map showing location of Sharm el Sheikh in Egypt and surrounding countries)

The language used within your body paragraph needs to vary in accordance with the directive words of the question. Here is a brief overview of the requirements of the different styles of geography questions:

QUESTION TYPE	LANGUAGE REQUIREMENTS
Explain	- Explain questions require you to relate cause and effect. - These questions require fewer in depth case studies but more brief facts and statistics that prove why factor x leads to outcome y.
Describe	- Describe questions require an in-depth understanding of case studies and illustrative examples. - To excel in these responses, you need detail in your essay which may come in the form of quotations from relevant academics, statistics or case studies.

Evaluate	- Evaluate questions require you to briefly outline a phenomenon and then make a judgement as to the value or effectiveness of that occurrence.
	- Evaluate questions are made effective through the use of words and phrases such as:
	  a. "Upon evaluation, this is/isn't an economically viable solution to the issue of ____"
	  b. "This exemplifies a highly effective and efficient strategy"
	  c. "Upon assessment this makes this strategy unlikely to be effective in the long term"

Concluding sentence making a final outline of the ideas addressed or providing an overall evaluative statement.

Note that the number of body paragraphs within your essay should be determined by the time you have to complete your response and the amount of material you deem necessary to answer the question. There is no clear rule about the amount of material that justifies a strong response. However, some questions such as:

> *Account for the changing nature, character and spatial distribution of mega cities. (20 marks)*

lend themselves to a three-body paragraph structured response. This would include a paragraph allocated to the nature, character and spatial distribution of megacities respectively, and the way that each is changing within the present socio-political climate.

Important notes about question words

Answering geography essays thoroughly is dependent on a clear understanding of what the question requires you to do. Confusion commonly occurs with questions such as:

> *Explain how locational factors have affected the nature and character of an economic enterprise.*

To answer this question correctly requires a clear understanding of the difference between nature and character:

Nature	In general, nature refers to the "what" of the enterprise or activity. This includes features such as size, shape and location.
Character	In general, character refers to the "how" of the enterprise or activity. This includes the way it operates such as the flow of goods and services, transportation routes and the import or export of goods.

Skills in Geography

Practicing and mastering skills in geography is a key determinant of a student's success within the subject. The skill section has had the least variability in terms of the difficulty level of questions over the years. This means that the multiple choice and short answer skills section are easy places to pick up marks. To master the skills section, I employed the following strategy:

1. Start early.

It is all too easy to leave skills to the last minute as you try to master the vast amount of content within the HSC syllabus. However, skills are an expertise that takes time to acquire. This means it is almost impossible to cram the study of skills . Starting from early in year 11 I decided to allocate one afternoon a week when I would sit down and study skills. Depending on the time that my other study tasks took or how close assessments were, this would vary from completing an HSC skills section, to answering all the syllabus skills questions. However, I promise that, in the long run, it takes less time to master skills if you do a little bit over a long period of time rather than crossing your fingers the night before.

2. Answer the skills dot points in the syllabus.

The skills that will be tested are clearly outlined in the geography syllabus. Therefore, I would recommend structuring your skills notes as follows:

SYLLABUS DESCRIPTION	EXPLANATION
Constructing cross section	1. Place a piece of paper along the line and mark the grid reference of the endpoints. 2. Mark each contour line that crosses the line and note its height. 3. Transfer the paper to a prepared grid and use the vertical scale to plot the heights of each point. Use the same horizontal scale as the map. 4. Join the points with a smooth curved line not a ruler. 5. Shade the area under the line to further emphasise the topography.

Example	HSC Geography 2017 Sample Answer Question 21a
	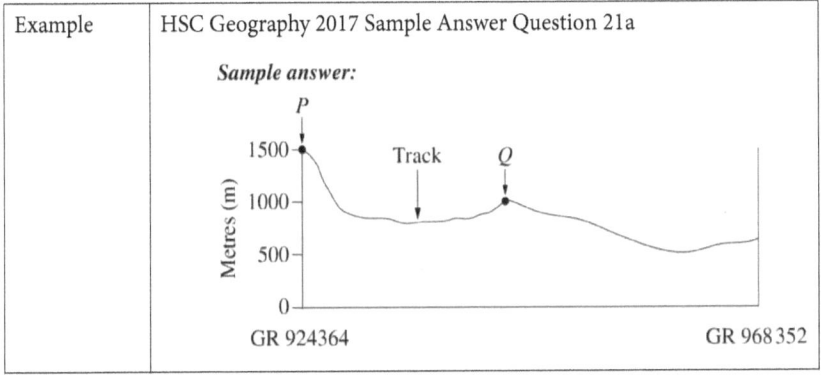

3. Practice makes perfect.

The best way to master skills is to practice them. I found that completing the skills sections in past HSC papers was the most efficient and effective means of studying. Once you have completed these papers, <u>marking your answers is crucial.</u> Completing past papers early allows you to identify your own areas of weakness. If you continually get the same type of question wrong, obtaining other resources, such as specifically designed HSC Geography skills workbooks, and completing the appropriate sections can be useful. As you get closer to the HSC, and your time becomes more precious, having a clear understanding of the types of questions you commonly get right and wrong allows you to designate your skills study time more efficiently in order to focus on your weaknesses, rather than continuing to reinforce your strengths.

CHEMISTRY

<u>The importance of the syllabus.</u>

In Science subjects, more than any other Year 12 subject, it is crucial that you thoroughly answer all the syllabus dot points. This includes being aware of the meaning of directive words (e.g. describe, evaluate, identify) and important definitions that are implicit to the syllabus requirements. It is important to have a thorough understanding of the syllabus in Chemistry because every year in the HSC there will be questions that are almost directly reworded from syllabus dot points. This enables NESA to test that your teacher has met the appropriate teaching requirements. Therefore, I would recommend structuring your study notes around the syllabus requirements. In addition, and importantly, you must also make sure you answer the syllabus dot points related to skills. An example of this method of writing study notes is as follows:

Syllabus wording	Assess the potential of ethanol as an alternative fuel.
Identify what the directive words ask for	Assess: provide points for an against a proposition and determine which side of the argument is stronger.
Key definitions and underlying theory	1. What is ethanol? Can you write a chemical equation for it and its combustion? 2. What is currently used as fuels? Can you write a chemical equation for their combustion?
Answer the dot point	1. Reasons why ethanol could serve as an alternative fuel 2. Reasons why ethanol is a poor alternative fuel 3. Assessment of potential (In HSC Chemistry it is crucial that you are seen to directly answer the question using the directives given. This means concluding with a sentence such as "Upon assessment ethanol has a high/low potential as an alternative fuel". The assessment you give depends on the points provided in the earlier part of the question.)

Past HSC question that related to this part of the syllabus	e.g. Outline TWO advantages and TWO disadvantages of using ethanol as an alternative fuel for motor vehicles. (HSC Chemistry 2017 Q28)
Things learnt from reading the marking criteria	a. "To outline" involves including more information than "identify" questions. Therefore, a proper explanation of each point was required to award full marks. b. Better answers included a chemical equation; for instance, the combustion of ethanol.

How to complete past papers so they are actually useful

A common piece of advice given to HSC students is "past papers, past papers, past papers". Whilst I agree with the sentiment of this advice, that increasing practice does improve marks, it is easy to spend hours completing past papers whilst gaining little from the experience. Consequently, I devised the following method for maximising after the benefit from completing past papers.

After completing the paper, I would **thoroughly work through the marking criteria**. It is easy to brush over this part. However, I learnt that often reading through the marking criteria is more valuable than completing the paper. This is because reading enough marking criteria teaches you to **think as if you were a marker**, so that when you approach a question you are able to process what a marker would be looking for to award your answer full marks. After reading through the marking criteria and identifying any errors, I would set up the following table:

Table showing errors from past HSC/ trial papers;

a. Paper and question number	b. Question	c. Reason that I got the question wrong (silly mistake/ skills deficit or unaware of content)	d. Sample correct answer (copied from marking criteria)	e. Topic area	f. Things I need to add to my notes in response.

Developing this table allowed me to do a number of things that truly contributed to my success:

1. Identifying trends in column e allowed me to choose what topic area required additional study time.

2. Column f allowed me to test how effective my study notes actually were. In addition, as a final piece of content review before the exam I would re-read column f to cement the pieces of content that were likely to be the most unfamiliar to me.

3. If I completed the past paper multiple times, I could determine whether I was repeating the same types of mistake. If this was the case, I would modify the way I completed papers and study accordingly. For instance, if I found column c consistently telling me that I was losing marks because of calculation errors, I would specifically dedicate the time remaining at the end of the paper to carefully checking and redoing any calculation questions.

4. Column d revealed questions that repeatedly came up in papers. If I noticed this, I would actually commit the sample answer to memory, given that I knew that there was a high chance that a similar, if not identical, question would come up in trials or the HSC.

Developing generic answer templates for questions.

Often students will complain that they lose marks in chemistry because they didn't know that they had to include something that was marked. The trick here is to know the specific requirements for each type of question that you may encounter in chemistry. Consequently, I would advise memorising these question formats and answering questions accordingly:

Question Type	Template answer
Evaluate	1. Provide a one-sentence evaluation, specifically using the word **evaluation**. e.g. "Upon evaluation the impacts of ___ have been primarily beneficial/detrimental to society and the environment"
Evaluate	2. If your evaluation is positive, to justify this evaluation the format becomes | Good | Bad | | --- | --- | | 3 or 4 points | 1 or 2 points | 3. If your evaluation is negative, to justify this evaluation the format becomes | Good | Bad | | --- | --- | | 1 or 2 points | 3 or 4 points | 4. To determine the number of points to include, the number of points (good and bad) should be equal to the number of marks in the question. **N.B** Any evaluation question worth more than 4 marks usually requires a form of chemical equation to justify your evaluation.
Discuss	1. Your introductory sentence should explain that you understand the requirements of the question. Discussion questions require you to show an understanding that the topic has both good and bad elements. You do not need to decide which side is stronger. e.g. The use of ethanol has a variety of impacts, both good and bad, on society and the environment.

| Explain | Explain questions are questions that require an outline of cause and effect. Therefore, the structure should be:
1. A logical sequence of the steps that occur to obtain the end result. Given that this is chemistry, to obtain the marks you should include chemical equations in each relevant step.
2. An outline of the end result. |
|---|---|

Sample "Explain" question

E.g. Question 26 (Sample Chemistry paper)

Explain how the pH of the propanoic acid solution would change if it was diluted. Include a relevant chemical equation in your answer.

What dilution does to the equilibrium systems	1. A weak acid will undergo a reversible reaction and only partially dissociate. $$CH_3CH_2COOH_{(aq)} + H_2O_{(l)} \rightleftharpoons CH_3CH_2COO^-_{(aq)} + H_3O^+_{(aq)}$$ 2. The propanoate ion is the conjugate base of a weak acid. Therefore, it has sufficient strength to react with water (hydrolysis) in the following equilibrium reaction $$CH_3CH_2COO^-_{(aq)} + H_2O_{(l)} \rightleftharpoons CH_3CH_2COOH_{(aq)} + OH^-_{(aq)}$$ 3. Le Chatelier's principle states that when a system in equilibrium is disturbed the system will shift to minimise the disturbance and establish a new equilibrium. 4. Dilution (the addition of water) disturbs the first equilibrium. In response, the equilibrium shifts to the right to favour the forward direction and to counter the increase in water. Consequently, the relative concentration of products increases, and reactants decreases. This initially causes the concentration of hydronium ions to increase. 5. The increased concentration of hydronium ions disturbs the second equilibrium system. Following Le Chatelier's principle, the system shifts to the right to favour the forward direction and to counter this increased concentration of hydronium ions. The relative

		concentration of products increases and reactants decreases. Consequently, the relative concentration of hydroxide ions increases.
The consequence for the final pH	1.	Since the concentration of hydroxide ions increases and pH = - log [H_3O^+] and pH+ pOH=14, this causes the pH of the system to increase.
	2.	Therefore, the system becomes more basic.

The importance of diagrams in chemistry

Chemistry is a subject where presenting information in alternative ways to the written form, in order to improve clarity, is looked upon favourably. Consequently, it is important that when completing past trial and HSC papers you observe the types of questions that demand diagrams and the requirements for the diagram to obtain full marks.

In general, here is an outline of the types of questions where diagrams are expected and an exemplar sample diagram. Of importance is that in order for a diagram to obtain full marks it **MUST be labelled.**

Type of question	Example diagram
Questions regarding intermolecular forces. These involve questions regarding; - Solubility - Entropy - Boiling points	Diagram showing solubility of ethanol in water: [Diagram showing ethanol molecule with non-polar part (H-C-C-C-C) and polar part (C-O-H) with $\delta+$ and $\delta-$ labels, interacting with water molecule (H-O-H with $\delta+$, $\delta-$, $\delta+$ labels) via dipole dipole bonding and hydrogen bonding]

| Experimental set up questions.
 - These involve all questions that relate to a practical that is syllabus mandated or that you are being asked to devise a method for. | 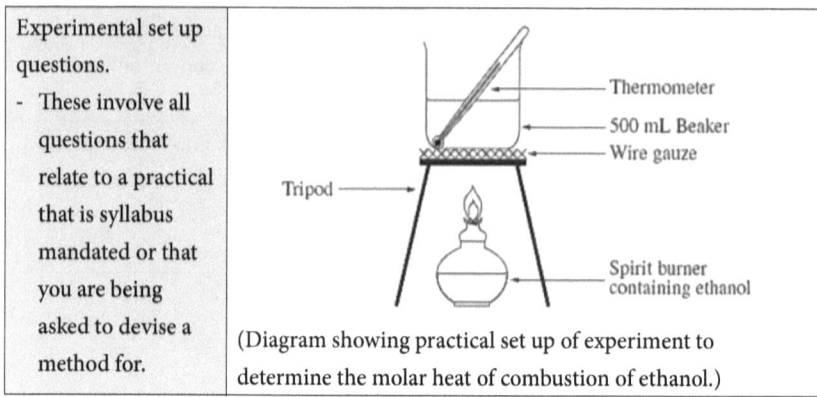
 (Diagram showing practical set up of experiment to determine the molar heat of combustion of ethanol.) |

Final notes

To conclude, here are some final tips for acing the HSC chemistry exam:

1. To create perfect chemistry answers, imagine you are a marker in the marking centre. Ask yourself: "If this is a **three-mark question, do I have three clear statements** that can be clearly allocated a mark each?" If you can't identify where you think the marks will be given, it is unlikely that the marker will be able to either. Learning how marks are allocated in HSC chemistry comes with practice. My best piece of advice is to read many marking criteria so that you get a clear understanding of how they are devised and operate.

2. READ THE QUESTION. Chemistry questions are notorious for having many components of a single sentence. This makes it easy to just give away marks because you forgot to clearly identify all the components of the question. My advice is to use **numbering notation** as you read the question in order to identify all the question requirements. See the following example:

   Sample Chemistry paper Question 21 (4 marks)

   Describe the changes that occur in both bonding and entropy when potassium chloride is dissolved in water. Support your answer with a labelled diagram.

This question requires you to do four things that you should identify before you begin writing:

   I. Description of **changes** in bonding for potassium chloride (**Change questions** require a description of BEFORE AND AFTER for all components of the system. Therefore, this involves an explanation of the ionic→ ion dipole changes that occur.)

   II. Description of **changes** in bonding for water (hydrogen and polar bonds between molecules→ ion-dipole bonds)

   III. Description of **changes** to the entropy of the system

   IV. **Labelled** diagram of all molecules involved.

3. Enjoy the subject! HSC Chemistry is difficult, but it is also a beautiful science and can be a whole lot of fun. Where else do you get to learn and understand everything from why the oil separates in your salad dressing to the total volume of gas in our universe? If you can enjoy this subject as much as I did, I promise it will become easier to study and your marks will improve.

I wish the best of luck!

HOW TO PUT THE STUDY IN LEGAL STUDIES

By Jenny Wang

> *"Why worry? If you've done the very best you can, worrying won't make it any better." – Walt Disney*

The HSC journey is a daunting one; one which brings much stress, anticipation and anxiety, but also one which can be extremely rewarding. My name's Jenny Wang and I attended Hornsby Girls High School. I graduated in 2018 with few specific life goals or ambitions. Despite my Asian heritage, I did *not* want to be a *doctor* or a *lawyer*; nevertheless, I still pursued academic excellence passionately.

I was always driven by the desire not to regret things. The thought of looking back at my HSC experience and regretting that I hadn't put in enough time and effort, or asked enough questions, was honestly terrifying. Every time I lost motivation, I would remind myself how this was the last push, the storm before the calm if you will.

General Advice – motivation, time management, balancing mental health and study, etc.

I got an ATAR of 99.80 and achieved a band 6 in all my units. I came the 4th in HSC Legal Studies and was the dux of my school in 2018. Looking at these results, you wouldn't think that I struggled with anxiety for over five years. I remember being scared witless in the years leading up to my HSC. If you're feeling the same, don't worry: you're definitely not alone. It happens to the best of us. The HSC journey is one that is mercilessly riddled with pitfalls and it is SO HARD to stay motivated, resilient and optimistic.

Due to my anxiety, I was seeing a psychologist regularly from Year 9, and had developed a vitally supportive relationship with a wonderful psychologist who compassionately and skilfully guided me through my HSC journey. And with her help, I collected a few tips, tricks and *apps* that actually assisted me to stay *more* composed than my friends when the HSC exams came around.

1. Say NO to procrastination

My main tip is **time tracking**. Basically, this means logging study hours for each subject. Now, at face value this does nothing to kick procrastination in the butt, *but* it does wonders to create a sense of achievement and purpose. When your timer is on, it holds you accountable. You can't and shouldn't be doing anything other than what you're logging! When you start procrastinating on YouTube etc., you've got to stop the timer. That means you're making a mindful decision to stop studying and give yourself a break. At the end of the week, month and year, it is so rewarding and satisfying to see how much time you've put into each assignment, task or subject, and it does wonders for your motivation.

This leads me to my second point.

2. Cling to your motivation

Maintaining high levels of motivation is more difficult than generally talked about. I thought I was alone in my slumps, but *everyone* struggles with this. Now this will sound kind of shallow but having pretty notes is quite important to keep your motivation up. If you type your notes up in Microsoft Word, I highly recommend using the page number headers and colour coding them to your subject. Trust me, it adds a little flair to your notes!

The "it's now or never" mentality also helps. You may be bored of school, sick and tired of the monotony and the seemingly never-ending commitments. But honestly, keep pushing because it will be over before you know it. Put up your favourite inspirational quote in your study area. You want to go through the HSC without looking back and regretting anything.

3. Stay organised!

A comprehensive filing system, time management and scheduling ahead are vital. I would always schedule my study blocks in the two weeks before exams. Here are my tips:

1. *Don't schedule specific time slots as it reduces the flexibility of your timetable.* Instead, I varied the sizes of my table 'cells' to correspond with the relative amount of time I would spend on the subject area. A larger box would mean a longer period of time spent and vice versa. This gives you a guideline whilst still allowing for flexibility.

2. *Be realistic.* Better to schedule less in a day and feel accomplished after having done extra, than to leave tasks incomplete and lose motivation.

In addition, keeping your notes in a comprehensive filing system is vital to staying organised and therefore allowing better and more effective preparation when exams come around. I would always advise making your own notes rather than buying or using others', as the note-making process is an effective way to consolidate your learning.

In my HSC year, I brought a binder with subject dividers, a binder hole punch and loose-leaf refills to school. I also had binders at home: one (or several) for each subject. When my school binder got full, I would unload the work sheets into the ones at home, keeping everything organised and collected in one place. This ensured that the note-making process, when it came to preparing for exams, was much more efficient.

Good luck! You can do it. Just keep pushing forward.

Love, Jenny.

	SUNDAY	MONDAY	TUESDAY	WEDNESDAY	THURSDAY	FRIDAY	SATURDAY
30 September – 6 October	*Mathematics*: 2014 HSC paper	*Chemistry*: work on Industrial Chemistry Notes	*Mathematics*: 2003 HSC paper				*Mathematics*: 2014 HSC paper
		English: start memorising Module B	*Modern History*: start/fully memorise Ho Chi Minh	*Modern History*: continue memorising Ho Chi Minh/work on Essays		*English*: practice Paper One Question One	*Legal Studies*: finish Human Rights and start memorising Family
	Chemistry: work on Industrial Chemistry notes	*English*: fix Brother and Sisters paragraph/other		*Chemistry*: finish/study Industrial Chemistry	*English*: watch The Hours/better Module A	*Modern History*: start memorising Indochina	*English*: continue memorising Module B
7 October – 13 October	*Maths Extension 1*: 2002 HSC paper	*Chemistry*: 2015 HSC paper	*Legal Studies*: past HSC multiple choice since 2011	*Modern History*: continue memorising Indochina/start memorising Germany	*English*: better AOS, Module B, Module C notes	*Mathematics*: past HSC paper	*English*: start memorising AOS and Creative
		English: start memorising Module A	*English*: start memorising Module C			*Legal Studies*: continue memorising Crime and World Order	*Legal Studies*: continue memorising Family and World Order
	Legal Studies: start/fully memorise Human Rights	*Legal Studies*: start memorising Crime	*Legal Studies*: start memorising World Order	*Maths Extension 1*: past HSC paper	*English*: start memorising Module A		

				THURSDAY		
				BIRTHDAY LUNCH		

(My study timetable in the lea- up to the HSC exams which started on the 18th of October [which also happened to be my birthday!]. Keep in mind I still set aside time for myself [note: BIRTHDAY LUNCH] and wrote an inspirational, albeit cheesy, quote to myself to keep motivation levels high.)

130 / Catch up with top achievers: 2019 HSC edition

Using a diary also helped. Whether it be an online, digital diary or a paper diary, scheduling when exams are on or when assignments are due is vital to staying organised.

Now, onto Legal Studies

I loved HSC Legal Studies. It was challenging and significantly broadened my understanding of societal issues and concerns. It enhanced my appreciation of and, in many cases, brought forth frustration at, the inherent flaws within the judicial system. It also inspired my desire to pursue criminology at university. My option topics were World Order (which I loved) and Family (which I also loved), but I'm sure my tips can apply in general situations regardless of which option topics you're doing.

Some general advice

Before I start, a heads up: there are no shortcuts or easy ways to study for Legal Studies. There may be tips and tricks to enhance your note-making skills, but at the end of the day, *YOU* need to put in the effort to memorise quotations, dates, legislation and arguments for each of your case studies. Knowing your case studies back to front will also ease some of your nerves before the exam. But trust me, you definitely get back what you put in.

Okay, onto the general advice:

1. *Know the themes and challenges of the syllabus well.* Using the terminology of the syllabus appropriately in your short answers and long responses is a great way to show your depth of understanding. It signposts to the marker that you understand the syllabus and that you're addressing the given question through an HSC Legal Studies framework. Also, it allows you to link smaller issues back to the bigger picture, i.e. the legal system's central goals and core values. Ask yourself: what does the legal system want to achieve? (This is expressed in the themes and challenges.) Is it successful in achieving this goal?

2. *Do not overthink multiple choice questions.* This applies to all subjects but particularly in Legal Studies; overthinking the question will result in the wrong answer. Go with your gut; your well-informed and well-prepared gut ;-).

Make sure you have a clear evaluation or judgement in your long responses. Don't be afraid to be explicit and strong minded. As long as you support your argument with relevant quotations, details and legislation, the marker will accept your viewpoint. However, it is recommended that you do not treat issues as 'black and white.' The legal system is complex and multifaceted, so it is important to include BOTH advantages and disadvantages when discussing any legal mechanism. Take these statements for an example:

> *Imprisonment is a largely ineffective means of punishing offenders and achieving justice as it is disproportionately expensive and does little to limit recidivism. It should be acknowledged, however, that imprisonment is necessary to incapacitate seriously violent offenders which may otherwise pose a significant harm to the community.*

See how I maintained a somewhat balanced stance. The legal system is the way it is for a reason. It can't be all bad. Note also how I linked the issue of imprisonment back to the legal system's major goal of 'achieving justice' as expressed in the themes and challenges. I also implicitly tied in the issue of 'compliance and non-compliance' by discussing recidivism. Notice as well how I clearly stated my argument and briefly outlined my supporting sub-arguments. More on that later.

Keeping up-to-date with the News can be extremely useful in allowing you to form your own judgements about the effectiveness of the legal system. Read media articles and understand its role in promoting efficacy and justice.

Exam preparation and note-making skills

I have mentioned A LOT about note-making . Here's how I actually did it:

- Restrictions on travel and behaviour
- Mandatory participation in rehabilitation and education programs

---

Case Study
Imprisonment
Imprisonment is a custodial sentence which involves the full-time detention of a convicted offender in a correctional facility. The *Crimes (Sentencing Procedures) Act 1999 (NSW)* states that *"a court must not sentence an offender to imprisonment unless it is satisfied…that no penalty other than imprisonment is appropriate."*

Advantages:
- Imprisonment effectively incapacitates an offender, protecting the community against any crimes they may wish to commit within the terms of their prison sentence and allowing time for rehabilitation to be achieved.

Disadvantages:
- Some offenders are being imprisoned for relatively minor crimes, unsustainably increasing prison populations.
  - In January 2016, the NSW prison population hit a record of 12, 121, rising 12 percent from the last year (SMH).
  - A larger prison population denotes a strain on prison resources as rehabilitation schemes which run in gaols become increasingly unavailable to the majority of inmates.
- Statistics have suggested that imprisonment is largely ineffective at reducing rates of recidivism
  - About 48 percent of inmates leaving NSW prisons return within two years (2014-2015 Productivity Commission)
  - Conflicts with community interests; imprisonment fails to fulfil its purpose in rehabilitating and specifically deterring the offender from further breaches of criminal law
- The effect on general deterrence is also limited
  - 1 to 2 percent decrease in rates of crime for a 10 percent increase in incarceration rates
- Expensive/costly
  - Costing the Federal government about $2.6 billion a year (SMH)

Non-Custodial Penalties

Non-custodial penalties: does not involve an imprisonment term or being taken into the custody of Corrective Services NSW. Examples include fines, cautions, community service orders etc.

Non-custodial penalties are more appropriate where the offence is at a lower level of seriousness. The *Crimes (Sentencing Procedure) Act 1999 (NSW)* allows for a diverse range of non-custodial penalties.

First of all, I firmly believe that making notes is an extremely useful study tool in the first place. It may be tempting to use other people's notes, but making your own is truly the best way of consolidating and condensing your knowledge.

You do NOT have to format your notes like I did (it took a LOT of time and effort, but I wanted to make my notes look pretty, haha) but it did help discern case studies from content for Crime.

- Case studies were in textboxes with broken lines.
- Definitions were in textboxes with solid lines.
- All other content for multiple choice was written as usual.

For case studies:

- First, I defined/explained what the issue/legal mechanism was.
- Where relevant, I identified the relevant legislation and what the legislation stated.
- In my notes, I didn't state an overall judgement of the mechanism's effectiveness. But in exams, I would first establish a clear judgment or argument before expressing my sub-arguments, which are comprised of advantages and disadvantages. This overall argument should be an informed judgement of how effectively the legal mechanism functions or how effectively the issue was addressed, depending on the nature of your case study.
- Ideally, each sub-argument should be evidenced with relevant quotes or statistics.

When studying for exams, I would pretty much memorise my case studies (not necessarily word for word; but when you read something enough, you *will* recall the words you originally used in an exam) and all the content in my notes. Here are some pointers:

- Be selective with your content for crime. Ask yourself, could you ask a multiple-choice question on this?
- Highlighting helped for me, but the most important thing is finding the study technique that works best for you. Draw mind-maps, use flash-cards, read something over and over and cover it to test your knowledge…there are so many ways to memorise content. Read it out-loud even, record yourself and then listen to yourself again.

The best thing to do when memorising content is to space it out in smaller chunks. Don't try and remember it all in one day. If you look at my study timetable above, you'll see that I memorised different topics on different days. Spacing out your study helps a lot with absorbing it.

Exam techniques

Being efficient and effective is the key to success in a Legal Studies exam. Here are some general tips:

1. Know your **syllabus** back to front, especially the themes and challenges! The themes and challenges act as a great frame of reference when identifying whether the goals of the legal system are being met. Some key issues are compliance, recidivism and whether the rights of offenders, victims and society are appropriately balanced. When you 'name-drop' these terms correctly, it shows the marker that you greatly understand the overall goal of the criminal justice system.

2. Speaking of name-dropping, name-drop **key terms in the question** throughout your essay to signpost to the marker that you are answering the question. Don't go off topic and make sure that your argument is clear. You can say something like this:

Q: Examine the impact of post sentencing considerations on the achievement of justice.

> *Post sentencing considerations* are *hugely important* in upholding the *rights of offenders, victims and society* and ensuring that the *purposes of punishment* such as rehabilitation and reducing recidivism are *satisfied*.

Notice how I

- identified the syllabus point, theme and challenge that the question is asking;
- formulated a clear and concise judgement or argument; and
- formulated my own criteria for what "the achievement of justice" looks like, whilst also citing other themes and challenges; this is an elaboration on the question.

3. My teacher heavily advocated **planning** before starting your essay. It can be as easy as mapping out which issues you want to target! Even with something as simple as that, you have already given yourself more time to carefully consider the question and decide which issues best relate. It is better to do this than to start writing about an issue and only realise half-way through that it doesn't really suit the theme and challenge which is the syllabus dot point identified in the question at all. (And trust me, I'm speaking from experience.)

4. For Crime **multiple choice**, usually the first answer that pops into your head is the correct one (that is, if you have prepared well to begin with). So, go with your gut!

Writing an essay

At this point I've already dropped a few tips and tricks on how to write a killer essay, but here are some more sure-fire ways to slay your essays.

Introduction

Like I've said before, **answer the question explicitly**. Don't assume that the marker will figure out your argument for themselves.

Identify the **themes and challenges (T&C) and the syllabus points or sections** that the question draws upon. Address these in your introduction and use these throughout your essay. These provide a great framework for your criteria as to what a good or bad legal mechanism is; e.g. for Crime, legislation should encourage compliance (T&C), effectively balance the rights of victims, offenders and society (T&C), and reduce recidivism (syllabus dot point – purposes of punishment) etc.

Explain any relevant terminology and introduce relevant legislation. (This may not be necessary or appropriate, depending on what essay question you get.)

Legal Studies does not require very long introductions. Keep your introduction short and concise.

<u>Body Paragraphs</u>

Divide your body paragraphs into issues you want to discuss. For example, in a post sentencing considerations essay, you may write one paragraph each on the following issues: parole, continued detention and deportation. Generally, in Crime I would use 3 to4 issues, and in Option Topics I would use 4 to5. It is ALWAYS better to talk in depth about a few issue than to talk about more issues.

In your body paragraphs:

- Define any relevant terminology and introduce relevant legislation. What are the aims of this legislation? Is it successful? Establish a judgement on a legal mechanism's effectiveness.

- Advantages/Pros and the supporting evidence can be introduced as follows:

    According to a BOCSAR report released in 2014,...

    48.6 per cent of unsupervised offenders had re-offended in a period of 12 months compared with 43.6 per cent of those released on parole (BOCSAR 2014)

- Then explain how/why this statistic/quote substantiates your argument.

- Disadvantages/Cons and the supporting evidence. Then explain how/why this supports your argument. It is great if you can link this to/use similar words as your argument/judgement to give the paragraph cohesion.

- Summary sentence and argument given what you have discussed (usually this means that the argument is more specific and will refer to your sub-arguments in more detail). For example:

    The introductory argument could be: Granting parole has the effect of enhancing community cohesion and reducing the offender's likelihood of reoffending.

The concluding argument could be: With adequate supervision and careful consideration on the part of the State Parole Authority, parole has the potential to be hugely effective at achieving justice by reducing rates of reoffending and facilitating rehabilitation outside of prison.

Conclusion

This is usually kept relatively short and often works to reiterate your argument and leave the marker with a clear impression of your overall judgement. Do NOT introduce new concepts in the conclusion.

Short answer responses

In Human Rights you will be asked to answer several short response questions. Here are some tips:

- You do not have to do an introductory sentence. Launch straight into your response.

- Have a clear structure and give a detailed response. Specific detail impresses the marker.

- It may also be useful to look at the Marking Criteria of previous short response questions in the HSC.

- Usually, the standard approach is to define and provide an example or argument for every mark allocated to the question.

Finally, I leave you with my favourite quote:

> *"Why worry? If you've done the very best you can, worrying won't make it any better." – Walt Disney*

Or, in other, less eloquent words, don't worry. If you're trying your best, there isn't much else that anyone can ask of you. Your best is enough. You can do it, and good luck!

SURVIVING AND CONQUERING HSC GENERAL MATHEMATICS

By Lucinda Krek

My name is Lucinda Krek. I completed my HSC at St Luke's Grammar School in Dee Why in 2018, and with my score, I achieved first place in the state for General Mathematics. I have always prided myself on being a hard-working and passionate student, with the hopes of eventually having a career in sports science. Speaking from my personal experience with the HSC process, I have outlined some tips, tricks, and advice which was of value to me – I hope that it can be helpful for you, too!

My personal school experience

I am extremely fortunate to have had such an incredible school experience. It was an excellent environment to be in, and my teachers and my year group were all very supportive throughout my time in high school!

In addition to my support system, I always sought out to do my absolute best. With that, I am able to address my strengths as well as weaknesses. I am not a creative thinker; I struggled to come up with original ideas that would stand out to teachers, and often required guidance from my peers when required to invent ideas. However, when math is concerned, I excelled. Therefore, English ended up being my worst HSC subject, and General Mathematics being my best. This simply demonstrates that everyone has a strong and a weak subject.

In regards to General Mathematics, I was discouraged by the level of difficulty in the Year 11 material, which led me to dread attending class. Finding the content challenging, I spent a lot of time outside of class reviewing materials to attain average results. At this point, with advice from my teachers and the Math Department, I decided I would benefit from taking General Mathematics. Initially, I struggled with the content. After a couple of weeks of practice questions, the content became easier to understand, allowing for math to become one of my favourite subjects to study.

Overall, every student has a different experience from others throughout their HSC; this highlights the importance of never comparing your experience to your peers. Personally, I found HSC to be a lot less difficult and stressful than it is said to be, as I was heavily prepared thanks to the way of teaching and examining throughout high school.

Stress and motivation

"Stress" and "Motivation": two of the most common things I heard about during my HSC experience, and hence, some of the most important issues to address.

Stress

Throughout my whole high school experience, I would overly stress about small tasks and assignments. Once I had then completed and submitted the work, I would pity myself for the stress I put myself through to get it done, after realizing the **excessive stress wasn't worth it!**

Once I realized this, I was determined to try my best throughout the final year of my schooling without having to unnecessarily stress. To achieve this, I had the mindset that...

Good results are important, but not as important as my mental health

Prioritizing my mental health led to Year 12 being the one in which I experienced the least amount of stress, which therefore had a great impact on my results in a positive way. Some **ways I dealt with stress** include:

- Whenever I felt overwhelmed, anxious and stressed out, I would remove myself from the study place or task at hand for 10 to15 minutes (even longer if needed) and come back when my mind was fresh and clear. This enabled effective study as otherwise the stress would cloud my mind and lead to unproductiveness.

- Whenever I was stressed over a specific part of the math's syllabus, straight away I would talk to my teacher and try to understand it better to diminish the worry and anxiety of not knowing the point of the syllabus.

- Right before entering the exam room, I would rarely talk to my friends about the syllabus or anything to do with the exam, as this would make me second guess what I knew, making me doubt myself and stress even more.

- When sitting and waiting for the beginning of the exam , I would take deep breaths and reassure myself that I knew the content and I had done all I could up until that moment.

Overall, the most important advice I could give is simply this: don't stress too much over the HSC. I know this is easier said than done and I highly disliked it when past students were telling me this, but to my surprise, I found it true.

Unfortunately, it is certain that most students will experience stress in their year of HSC. Stress is inevitable; however, some stress in a controlled manner can be beneficial, as it indicates that you care and motivates you to complete the work and do well.

Motivation

Throughout my high school career, I was highly motivated and always set out to exceed the expectations set by my teachers as well as the goals I set myself.. This mindset and dedication to my studies allowed me to maintain a position at the top of my year for both General Mathematics and PDHPE. By setting a goal and making a plan to attain it, I was able to maintain motivation, which led to my achievement of the first rank in the state for General Mathematics and the third for PDHPE.

The most important tips I used to stay motivated include:

- Set **GOALS:** This could be a certain ATAR or exam result, allowing you to be motivated to work towards something specific.

- Be motivated to achieve great results for your own benefit and satisfaction: Whenever I achieved good results, it was always an amazing feeling, and I motivated myself to keep trying and uphold these results, and do even better the next time.

- I would constantly ask myself, *"Am I proud of the amount of work or the quality of the work I have completed?"* If I wasn't, this would motivate me to study more or improve my work. So, ask yourself these questions regularly.

- **PLAN**! Organize and plan what you need to study, whether it is for the next day or for the whole upcoming week. This stops procrastination and motivates you to start, as it indicates what and when you need to study.

- When feeling very unmotivated during study, choose favourite or familiar topics for a period of time. This will boost your confidence and motivate you to keep studying for longer.

Overall, don't be disheartened if you are feeling unmotivated throughout the year; it is inevitable at some points, just as I experienced periods when didn't want to start that assignment or begin studying the topic I didn't understand.

However, by using the ways outlined above, my motivation would return. Throughout the year, you will discover more ways of your own to keep yourself motivated!

MY MATHS STUDY TIPS

1. Think of studying for General Mathematics as a 'break' from other subjects.

Before you completely laugh and brush past this tip, hear me out. Within your other subjects, whether it may be English or something else, you have to think and write down thousands of words and ideas, which, for me, became extremely tiring.

Studying for math allowed for a break from the tiresome hours thinking of thesis, writing essays and memorising content, as there was a specific method and approach in each subject.

Therefore, whenever I felt overwhelmed by the content from my other subjects, especially English, I would complete a couple of math questions.

2. Don't just rely on the textbook.

Use other resources! Throughout my entire math study, I barely ever used my text book. The only time I would use it was during class or when my teacher assigned homework from it. Personally, I found the questions unhelpful for exam preparation, as they weren't 'exam style'. However, they could be useful to learn the concept of the topic.

3. Complete ALL the past papers you can find, and allow them to act as an indicator of what you do and don't know.

There is an abundance of past papers that could be very helpful. These could be past school exams, past HSC papers found online or from other schools.

My biggest advice for using past papers is to **NEVER DO IT WITH OPEN BOOK**! It is easy to get into the habit of flicking through questions and only completing the questions you know how to do. This is easy, BUT it will not benefit you in any way.

I completed them as if they were a test, which allowed for my exam techniques to be improved. Once completed I would mark it and highlight the questions I had got wrong or had difficulty with. After that, I would practice those topics I found difficult or got wrong to better understand the method.

4. Once you know and are confident with certain questions, move on!

If you keep completing questions that you know how to do, you are not going to improve your maths skills at all. Therefore, you need to focus on what you are struggling with.

5. When feeling unmotivated or unable to focus, do some questions that you know how to do.

I know this contradicts my last tip, but when I was feeling unmotivated or procrastinating, in order to lift my spirits, it was very helpful to complete a couple of questions on topics that I knew how to do. Then I would attempt to tackle harder topics, and then once again a topic I could do, to finish my study on a high note with.

6. Once in a while, have 'FUN' study days.

You've probably never heard 'fun' and 'study' in the same sentence, but it can be made possible!

To do this, make a whole day out of it, grab a couple of friends, go out for breakfast or lunch, then go to your school or local library and study either together or independently. It may not be the most productive day, but you would still study a great amount and it allows for a break within the boring and tiresome routine, meanwhile creating a better relationship with studying!

7. Don't study for long periods without breaks.

Throughout my studies, I found it challenging, unrealistic, and counterproductive trying to maintain focused for multiple hours at a time. An alternative method which I found effective was to spend 20 to 30 minutes of uninterrupted study time with concentration, and then allow myself a short break to process the information which I had just reviewed.

Notes and Organisation

Writing notes for General Mathematics felt like a waste of time. All the needed equations are on the formula sheet, making it unnecessary for them to be memorized.

However, if I ever needed to write notes on a certain topic that I was struggling with, it would be formatted as the following:

TOPIC:

EQUATION:

QUESTION AND DEMONSTRATION:

PRACTICE QUESTIONS:

Additionally, to ensure I was organized, I used a study timetable to plan what subjects and syllabus points I needed to review for the upcoming week. It was essential that I keep this timetable flexible, allowing changes easily if I needed to study another subject or syllabus point.

Specifically, when organizing my study for math, I would determine the parts of the syllabus I needed to study.

To remain organized throughout the entire school year, I ensured I would complete given tasks or homework as soon as I received it.

Exam Advice and Technique

1. Don't overcomplicate the question.

Think simply and logically. Some of the questions are designed to trick you by looking harder than they actually are. Don't be tricked!

2. Time yourself well.

Haste leads to mistakes. In order to avoid rushing to finish, you must be wary of the time throughout the exam to ensure you aren't falling behind.

3. Make sure you have left enough time to complete the last questions.

The last couple of questions are commonly the hardest and take the most time to complete, Therefore, you need to ensure that there is sufficient time for them to be completed as they are worth the most marks.

If you can't manage your time, it may be worth completing a couple of the hardest questions at the beginning of the exam to ensure you have them covered; however, test this with past papers and work out what you prefer.

4. If you have time, always double (or triple) check your answer.

It is necessary to check your answer or any mistakes made within your working out. My personal HSC experience shows that there were many small mistakes I had made throughout my working out, which made the answer wrong. Luckily, I double checked all my answers, fixed the mistakes made , and avoided errors.

5. HIGHLIGHT!

The most important exam technique is to highlight all the important numbers and key words in the question; this ensures you don't miss any part of the question that could change the answer completely!

6. Know your formula sheet well!

Knowing the right equation well will save you the much needed time for the question that may give you the much needed marks.

7. BREATHE before you start a new question.

This allows for a brief pause and a fresh mindset to complete another question.

8. Never give up on a question.

Firstly, have a go, and if you are struggling and wasting time just staring at the question, move on and come back to it.

When a question is left blank, that is a guaranteed 0 mark; however, if you have an attempted go at the question, you may be able to score a mark by having something correct in your working out.

9. If you have the choice, don't leave your exam early!

I know from personal experience that you just want to get out of the exam room as soon as you can, but I advise you not to! Use ALL the time you are given because within a math exam, you can never check your answer too many times. In my own HSC exam, I had finished with just over an hour to go, and that allowed me to have a complete check of my answers multiple times. Even though I had the chance to leave early, I kept checking up until the last minutes of the exam.

Final Words

My final advice would be to not let the HSC take over your life!

I believe that it is incredibly important to take time to enjoy all of the fun and exciting parts of your final year of high school, and work hard to maintain balance throughout the HSC period. Throughout the entire HSC process, keep in mind that your best is your best, regardless of how that matches up against your peers. HSC is a very short period of time in the grand scheme of high school, so keep in mind that at the end of the whole process you are not your results. Regardless of what score may appear on paper – the results don't define the potential you have for achievements after high school!

HOW TO ACE MUSIC 1

By Varun Mahadevan

A Snapshot of Me

- Girraween High School Graduate
- Guitarist
    - Repertoire (For any advanced guitarists looking for suggestions):
        - Every Piece Matters – PLINI
        - Champagne – POLYPHIA
        - The Nomad – CALUM GRAHAM
        - Bullet in the Head – ANDY JAMES
- HSC Mark: 100
- Encore Nomination
- 2nd in NSW for 2018 in Music 1
- My plan: As of 2019, I am commencing a Bachelor of Commerce / Bachelor of Music at UNSW. The B.Mus. may not really come as a surprise, given my enthusiasm for music, my eventual career goal.

- My favourite Motto:

    Polaris – **'Lucid'**
    I found my love and let it kill me"

- Quite self-explanatory, – this reveals the extent to which we should pursue our goals and dreams. Polaris wrote about being in a band with 'Lucid' and so this quote happened to align with my personal aspirations.

- Whilst it may seem inane to compare chasing ambitions to thriving in the HSC, the HSC really is a test of your limitations. By using a similar level of effort in your HSC as you would to achieve your ambitions, you will notice that not only will you thrive, but your confidence in achieving your ultimate goals will also rise remarkably.

My Experience in Music 1 in a nutshell

Honestly, Music 1 was the most enjoyable part of my high school experience. By that, I don't mean the subject itself; I mean the experience of growing as a musician alongside your musically gifted peers, all of whom are incredibly talented. It really forms a strong sense of camaraderie within your class, as you all watch each other develop aural, compositional and practical skills; all the while you have the unending support of your teacher. Music 1, for me at least through Year 11 and Year 12, was the subject where the class didn't feel like a class.

That's what Music 1 should feel like. As clichéd as it may sound, Music 1 should not and most likely will not feel like an amalgamation of content and skills being hurled at you like almost all your other subjects. It's a genuinely fun subject, and although there are stressful situations, it is the period or double period within your day you most look forward to.

How to Score High in Music 1

As you probably already know (unless you're still in Year 10 and are thinking of whether to do M1) you have one Core performance. This is a mandatory performance. Even if you prefer compositions or the aural analysis and pedagogical allures of Vivas, you must do at least one performance, and this Core performance is worth slightly more than each of the three electives you choose. So, the obvious advice I'll give here, and I'm sure your teachers and possibly even your music tutors would have already told you, is to nominate your strongest piece for it. Your strongest piece should also naturally be the one you are most confident about, so be sure to carefully pick your repertoire in order to show yourself off to your best ability.

Remember, in order to score as high as possible you want to show off to your markers with your Core performance and the three electives – whether it be your compositional, pedagogical or performing skills is up to you. However, make sure that within each elective it fits the marking criteria for a work at Band 6.

In what follows I'll distinguish what you should be aiming to show within your performance to make sure that it reaches that Band 6. (Most of the Music 1 cohort will be doing four performances, so I'm going into specific details for the criteria points. If you are choosing either composition/s or Viva/s, you MUST analyse the key words in the top band criteria to understand what they're expecting of you for each point.)

Performance

- Technical Fluency
    - Essentially, they want you to just show off what you can do.
- Stylistic Understanding
    - You need to be aware of your use of dynamic and expressive contrast.

- It'd also help you a lot if you were able to show a wide range of stylistic contrasts as well as careful articulation to show you have a grasp on the style of your musical piece.

- Understanding of Solo/Ensemble Techniques
    - Unless you're a pianist, the rule of thumb is that you have at least one ensemble piece.
        - This is so the markers can see that you are proficient within both solo and ensemble settings, as well as that you are able to understand ensemble roles and harmonies within an ensemble.

- Personal Expression
    - This is HOW you perform. This is quite possibly one of the dividers between a Band 5 and a Band 6 performance; for this sake markers are going to be scrutinising the way in which you perform.
        - Make sure that you're moving around if you can stand.
        - Make sure you're visibly 'feeling it' if you're sitting whilst playing.
        - Lastly, make sure you make eye contact with the markers here and there to engage with them.
            - Even if you don't lock eyes, they'll see that you're at least making an effort to engage.
    - I can't stress enough how important it is that you MUST be conscious of personal expression while you're performing.
        - One way to practice this is to just film yourself at home, or perform in front of a mirror. By doing so you can gauge your own mannerism and your need to improve your expression in order to reach the Band 6.

Aural

Now that's the externals covered for the major that we do. The actual Music 1 exam, i.e. Aural Skills, may weigh considerably less than the major; however, it is still important to do well in this both internally and in the externals to ensure a Band 6. My music teacher, Mr Jason Wajzer, always said [regarding doing well in aural] that "You're at the mercy of the paper".

This is undeniably true. No matter how much you're practicing past papers and analysing your own songs, you'll never know how hard, or easy for that matter, the excerpts are going to be to analyse, let alone what the question demands from you.

The best way to prepare yourself for the aural exam is honestly just to do one practice paper a week, straight up. If you're making a habit of doing at least parts of one paper a week, you're not only going to see that your analysis becomes better, but you'll realise how much you are expected to say in your response.

Remember, for aural – Quality always outweighs Quantity. Even if there is a lot to talk about holistically, you must make sure you're actually answering the question without repeating yourself. Markers will see through all the 'waffle' if all you are doing is just rewriting one point over four or five different points. I would consciously apply the following rules to make sure that I'd achieve higher marks in each question.

These key points will indicate HOW, in your practice, you should approach the questions, including the multiple concepts and more advanced questions:

- Underline or highlight what exactly the question is demanding.
    - This way you're actually distinguishing what you SHOULD be looking out for to avoid overlooking it when listening.

- Give the first listen to just take mental notes and get a feel for the excerpt.
  - You don't need to write during the first playing.
    - As long as you've got mental notes of some key areas to talk about, you should consider it a successful first listen.
- Use two pages for each question as a means to separate the concepts you're analysing.
  - Especially in a question with multiple concepts, by doing this you let the marker know easily which is which concept to mark.
- DRAW DIAGRAMS.
  - It can't be stressed enough that diagrams make explanations so much simpler. With diagrams you can write less to explain.
  - Diagrams also show that you're using higher order thinking to visualise what you hear.
    - Just draw whatever you hear. Often, you'll get the mark for being close, unless you specify and it's way off.
  - If you don't answer a Duration, Texture or Pitch question without diagrams, you're automatically going to get a lower mark.
- Learn your theory and apply it. Using technical music terms as opposed to describing in common terms shows your higher order thinking skills and more advanced knowledge.

Practice and Performing

A major help for me which allowed me to do so well in Music 1 was my extremely supportive and tight-knit class. I understand that there may be classes that aren't too close, but seeing your peers and classmates as your friends and teammates instead of competitors for internal ranks will ultimately be a great aid. Your teachers will probably have said to work together as a cohort, and in Music 1 this is essential. Here's why:

- Using each other for feedback after a performance or just practice gives you constructive criticism from someone that isn't your teacher and doesn't play your instrument. This is extremely beneficial as they understand the nervousness you're facing and will be as helpful as possible.

  There is one important tip: suggest what your peer could do to improve, rather than tell them what they should do.

- Performing in front of your class regularly builds up your confidence of helped me overcome my. prepares,.

- It boosts the classes morale seeing how talented everyone else is. will .

Major Work Practice Schedule

I'll be frank here. You need to practice as much as you can. The four songs you play, whether you're doing vivas or compositions, you will absolutely hate by the time you've reached your trials, but you have to make sure you're practicing on a regular basis. Personally, I taped a performance box to give myself room to move around while I practiced my repertoire start-to-finish. The point of that was to make myself conscious about my movement and my expression. I understand it'll be different for others, depending on their instruments; however, you have to ultimately decide what'll work for you.

Final Tips

Honestly, just have fun. Pick songs which are challenging to perform or analyse; compose what you enjoy but what you've also always wanted to experiment with. Music 1 isn't a hard subject if you put in the hard yards. I had a blast, but the success I achieved did not come with laziness. My final piece of advice is to make sure you're aware of your musicality but have a clear direction and vision of what you CAN achieve by the time your assessments come around internally and ultimately your externals. Whether it be learning a new technique, playing unusually fast, composing with a certain complex motif or analysing abnormally, you need to be aware of what you can currently do and what you can achieve in the near future. Realism will ground you and can aid you to ascertain that coveted Band 6.

MAJOR KEYS TO MUSIC SUCCESS

By Belinda Thomas

> "The question isn't who's going to let me; it's who is going to stop me." – Ayn Rand

You can carry a tune, you'd take AMEB examiners in a fist fight, you don't stop flexing your perfect pitch -- you've chosen HSC music. You don't know what you've signed up for when that first chord of that first contemporary Australian composition hits you. Unless you're lucky enough to be infatuated with that incomprehensible, impenetrable dissonance, there will undoubtedly be moments of questioning.

But isn't this what you're meant to be doing? Aren't you a music kid?

Herein lies my first piece of advice: choose HSC music. It's likely that you already have so many years of experience with music. So much of the course content is already under your belt and has been for years; something not every biology or extension Latin kid will be able to say.

Personally speaking, I wasn't a kid who knew how to study. I never put an abundance of effort into my studies, always found myself cramming the night (or morning) before, didn't have study plans, didn't know how I studied best -- but somehow I'd managed to survive my high school years relatively unscathed. I was creatively inclined, consequently likely a little insane, and very determined to live a life larger than academic infatuation. Emily Dickinson, the late-Romantic American poet with a reputation for feminism and paradox, asks, "why not have a big life?" -- and I think that sums it up quite nicely. Though I did receive unrequested pressure throughout my HSC journey, I wasn't going for any sort of stellar HSC success shown by numbers, but rather, I tried to complete a journey I'd be personally proud of and satisfied with.

Staying on-brand, my HSC year was a *complete* hot mess. A hot mess, but at least it was an orchestrated hot mess - literally. What I didn't realise until the end was that a lot of the things I thought were mistakes turned out to be times I played my cards well. Pushing whatever personal drama I had aside, I started the year rehearsing as leads in an operetta and a musical, became concertmaster of my school's orchestra, and decided to take the risky leap in choosing to use classical voice instead of violin for the performance component of Music 2, after being told explicitly pretty much – *not* to. Keeping the violin on for Extension meant I had to keep up two instruments , whilst trying to get my voice up to scratch in the first place.

That's my next bit of advice: completely inundate yourself in music. I know it seems utterly unrealistic to take on board a multitude of co-curriculars in this important year, but the stress-relieving capacity of music is priceless -- *and* it technically counts as study. Without my two productions, there's no chance I would've had enough time working on my voice. Of course, there were times when it put me on very thin ice, but persevering paid off.

It is true that our beloved creative arts courses have the innate demand for juggling many elements of the course; in our case - musicology, music skills, performance, composition, and very often extracurricular ensembles ... the list goes on. Something else you're going to have to deal with is having music dismissed by your peers as a course lesser than physics or extension maths is, but it'll be completely worth it when you snatch that 99 ATAR with your creative subjects. I'll always remember the shock on my friends' faces when they found out my ATAR, and all those tiresome physics study days they had spent while I'd been frolicking around suddenly flashed through their minds.

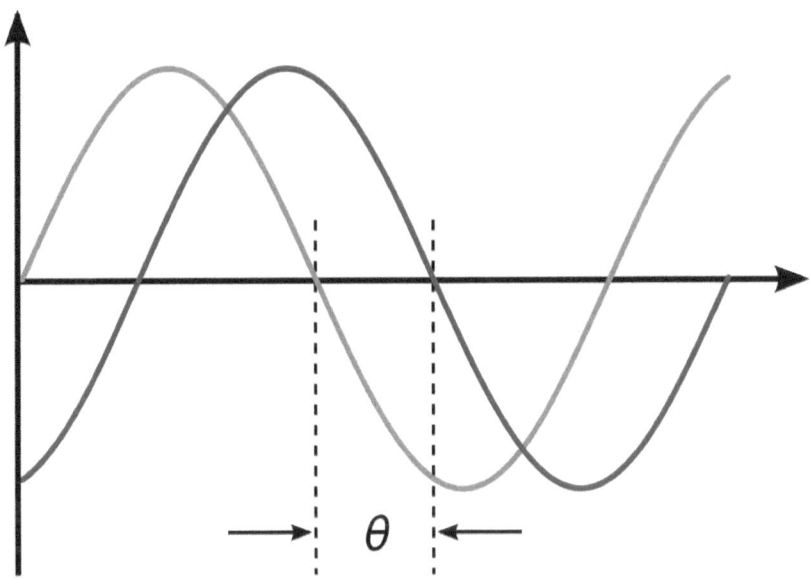

(Two sinusoidal waves offset from each other by a phase shift θ by Peppergrower, https://commons.wikimedia.org/wiki/File:Phase_shift.svg, Licensed CC BY 3.0 http://creativecommons.org/licenses/by/3.0)

In the midst of all the scaling jargon and egotistical physicists, know that you've made the right decision in choosing HSC Music. In my HSC year, Music 2 and Music Extension made up half of my four majors. *Yes*, four -- on top of Drama and Extension 2 English. I'd definitely been called crazy, but this decision was probably what contributed most, macrocosmically, to my HSC success. Though it seemed slightly insane at times, overall this arrangement meant that I was doing what I loved, what I was apparently good at, and something that I was willing to invest my time into. It also played itself out quite nicely as I could spread out my most stressful period, come time for trials and the actual HSC. Most of my major work assessments would come in one wave, and then in another wave my other subjects would come. Here's what I assume a physics diagram that shows how my stress levels and workloads pertaining to my subjects peaked with assessments, trials, then HSC. The red line stands for my subjects with major works, whereas the blue one for all the other subjects. This diagram took me an embarrassingly long time to find and I had to fact-check it with a friend who actually did physics, but it makes sense. The staggered peaks served me wonders in balancing out my HSC troubles.

Composition

The first thing I did, and probably what saved me the most, was getting my composition out of the way early. I managed to overcome procrastination and smash out a composition essentially over the Christmas holidays, prior to the real substance of the HSC year kicking in. Here's a crash course in tips for your 2:30 composition:

- Imitate (essentially, copy) the sound of all the Australian compositions you've been exposed to. Handpick an Australian trait for each element of music and push it.

- Pick an instrumentation you're very familiar with: this will definitely show when it comes to fleshing it out with instrumental techniques and tricks, and essentially crafting an innovative and highly creative composition.

- Develop one motif first -- that's all you need to wind 2:30 out of, and then twist it into ternary form.

- Choose a wild, and frankly, uncomfortable time signature. Time for odd numbers!

- Compose with purpose: choose a poem, message, speech, nursery rhyme. This will serve as a simple linking thread and assist you in creating something coherent.

- Try crazy things, but remember to save, save, save!

- Get as many people to listen to it as possible, and take all these opinions on board with a very significant grain of salt.

Something fantastic about Music is that your assessments don't see you sitting down in front of a sheet of paper for hours on end -- most of them, anyway.

Here is one more simple assessment tip: actually practice your sight-singing when you're told to. It counts as legitimately assessable content, and having an assessment that feels like a breeze does wonders!

Performance

For some, the most intimidating part of Music is performance, conveniently made compulsory. It's also the one part that you can't procrastinate and get off scot-free, so you *do* have to get on top of it. Fortunately, performing and practicing, though it can feel like a chore, is often significantly less infuriating than writing essays or doing math problems; remember this contrast with your alternative activities will serve you well.

Your core performance piece is likely going to be a struggle, with all the curveballs contemporary Australian art music loves to throw at you. Try and find one that you initially don't absolutely resent, and let it warm up to you as the year goes on and you learn more about it. I started the year with my core piece, Matthew Hindson's 'Little Chrissietina's Magic Fantasy,' a wicked quasi-electric violin firework show. A few weeks in, I threw out all the progress I'd made, and spent weeks searching for a new piece -- for voice. I was lucky enough to have access to the Australian Music Centre library and found the intriguing, fantastical Paul Stanhope piece I ended up using.

Something 'fun' to remember is that all these contemporary Australian composers are actually real people. This fact will give you that extra edge if you dare to reach out to them and ask questions about their compositions. If you're ever feeling that this core study is subpar or useless -- remember that this is the authentic music of the world you live in, the real sounds that surround you. This art music is as relevant as anything; these are the composers who are shaping and essentially creating the industry. Recently, I applied to audition for a choir which, I discovered, was conducted by no other than Paul Stanhope himself, whose music I had spent so long slaving over.

Musicology

This is undeniably not the most fun component of the course -- but there are definitely ways to reduce your workload. Initially for both your core and elective you'll study a plethora of pieces. But the ultimate goal is just to familiarise you with the characteristics and personality of the style of music. Out of the six or seven pieces per genre you study in class, you'll likely only need two (or three, tops) well-learnt pieces for your HSC Music journey.

The major grievance is writing music essays -- though it doesn't have to be a pain. You've done essay writing in other subjects, and this is where you get to steal absolutely every essay-writing technique you've accumulated in other subjects over the years. The objective is the same -- address the question, make a statement, then justify it with appropriate evidence; the only difference is that your quotations are music scores.

Though I was told to do copious past papers and essay questions, I didn't do many at all, maybe three practice essays in class and another one at home. How I got away with the bare minimum still continues to amaze me (protip -- become *best* friends with your teacher. I mean it.). Though I'm not advocating that you do it too, it's proof that there is definitely a way to work smarter rather than harder.

The musicology component of the course is engineered to teach you music in a specific way: to make you understand it via a breakdown of the six elements of music. Using these six elements to guide your study is therefore an immediate place to start. Next, though you've accumulated plentiful knowledge through your study and analysis of multitudinous set works, choose the two or three that you've either warmed up to the most, or which have the most obvious content to discuss. Across these pieces, you've hopefully got every single element of music covered once or twice. You can make study notes in a table to help you memorise relevant knowledge for exams or essays. Here's a sample:

Music 1900 - 1945 set works

	SET WORK 1 **Quartet for the End of Time - Messiaen 1941**	SET WORK 2 **Classical Symphony - Prokofiev - 1917**	SET WORK 3 **Pierrot Lunaire (Mondestruck) - Schoenberg 1912**
Background			
Pitch			
Duration			
Form/Structure			
Texture			
Timbre			
Dynamics & Expressive Techniques			

This gives you an essentially foolproof plan to cover any essay question thrown at you, with content covering every music element. The background information provides the context of each set work to strengthen your discussion. There's also information about the composer's decision in manipulating each element of music. Furthermore, it's ideal to use evidence that utilises more than one element of music; this lets you memorise less, and create a stronger, more intertwined argument. Also, remember to have a musical quote for every verbal analysis you use! Remember to keep your notes in this table succinct and relevant: less is more. Use techniques and evidence that are tangibly related to the era; here wider areas of study are necessary.

One of the works I ended up using in my 1900-1945 elective unit was Olivier Messiaen's *Quartet for the End of Time*. Though this composition wouldn't typically be what I listen to in my spare time, I knew that there'd be so much content in this work that could be easily plied into an essay, and that it'd be able to cover so many concepts of music even in one quote. Also, the piece has rich potential for making intellectual discussion look easy, interesting, and high-brow. Here's a part of the table I used to analyse Messiaen's use of pitch:

PITCH	
	• Modes of limited transposition; Mvt 6 = mode 6, made of 2 tetrachords around the tritone; centre of the octave = no distinct tonality emphasised, but not polytonal

	• Formed by symmetrical groups of notes, with the last note of each group being enharmonically equivalent to the first note of the following group - "at once in the atmosphere of several tonalities, without polytonality, the composer being free to give predominance to one of the tonalities"
	• Constant use of tritones as structural basis, part of cyclical nature; (bar 2.2, piano RH e flat-A natural, bar 3.1 G natural - C#, bar 3.3 LH F natural - B natural)
	• Birdsong - Experience as a synesthete (VI: expression of colours pertaining to change in instrumentation, fervid articulation) which is unique to Messiaen; written on the score ("bronze, copper")
	• Full range of register; interesting instrumentation as instruments of convenience.

What worked for me in my study was condensing the information as much as possible: synthesising every word (sometimes even every letter) allowed my brain to soak up as much raw information as possible. The condensed information could then be expanded and elaborated later on in an exam situation.

Here, you can see that the quote I've used is as simple as a scale -- but this scale ties into a sophisticated and innovative use of pitch that Messiaen has utilised and is therefore ripe for the analytical picking. As long as you can demonstrate that you've understood this manipulation of a music element, you can regurgitate this natural understanding to the demands of any essay question.

Additionally, using quotes straight from the composer allows for demonstration of great contextual understanding as well as lexical manipulation which makes your essay less tiresome to read. Or, see it as a shortcut to looking smarter -- why think of words yourself when Messiaen's already thought of them for you?

Exam technique

When it comes down to the wire, some exam technique can make all the difference in full-on Music exams. Here's how I approached an exam in both HSC and trials, which I also suggest to you.

- You need enough space to organise your sheets and sections in a way that's comfortable for you. If you have a small class, in exam conditions you can ask your teacher for a second desk to make things easier for you. I would set up two desks in an L shape, so that I had comfortable work space as well as an easily reachable spot to place my other scores when I didn't need them.

- When the recording starts, flip through the pages and scan them as fast as possible; read the composers and titles of the unseen pieces and vaguely establish in your mind which eras you're going to work with and which compartments of your brain with accumulated knowledge you're going to draw on.

- After you've skimmed at lightspeed, read the essay question at the back of the paper slowly -- read each word, read it with your finger pointing, mouth the words. Really get all those key terms into your brain, establish which eras of music you're working with and what knowledge you have to draw on, and quickly pick which set works are going to serve your point best. If you've prepared well, the elements of music should overlap slightly to give you a multi-faceted approach quickly.

- As soon as you can write, grab that manuscript and write down ALL of your quotes that you've memorised from all of your set works: the order becomes entirely redundant. Just write down those bars with each quote on a new line, and clearly label each quote at the start of the line of manuscript: Quote 1, Quote 2, and so on. Write these down in as much detail as possible, especially details that are relevant to the element of music you plan on using the quote to discuss. Writing down all my quotes (even ones I don't end up using) could save me an incredible amount of time, and prevent me from forgetting them (after I crammed them into my brain seconds before the exam started!)

    - *Please, please have decent handwriting for your music notes: make your clefs, note heads, stems, and accidentals super clear.*

- By now, the first set work has started playing. Clear your brain and get into the genre, era, and knowledge that is relevant to this recording. Baroque, Classical, Romantic, Contemporary -- you've accumulated enough knowledge over your years of music to become familiar with this genre and its quirks with each element of music. Address the question hyper-explicitly, naming direct manipulations of the element of music the question addresses, using clear dot-points (one dot-point for each mark the question is worth.)

- By the time you reach the dictation, hopefully you've finished writing down all your quotes in any extra space you've had with superfluous playings. Through years of aural training, I'd become quite comfortable with the idea of melodic dictations, so this part of the paper became a breathing point for me. I'm lucky enough to have perfect pitch, so I'd end up with a few unnecessary playings here. I'd use this extra handful of minutes to craft a quickfire essay plan and get stuck into my essay introduction. This would allow me to have my essay and its objective mulling over and processing in the back of my head for longer, even as I progressed through the rest of the paper. I'd continually skip back and forth through the paper to push through the essay, as I'd always known that 20 minutes would be nowhere near enough time to produce an essay with a decent argument and substantial analysis and evidence.

Finally, *please* remember to keep your mental health in check and take time to care for yourself. We creative souls are undeniably more susceptible to frangible mental states, and speaking up or at least expressing yourself somehow will be a necessary outlet to keep yourself afloat this year. You've probably heard this a million times, but your mental health will be particularly tenuous through the year. However, you're also lucky enough to have music as a beautiful pillar to support yourself, so use it as an outlet. Improvise with your instrument and see where it takes you. As clichéd as it may sound, get lost in the music. My mental health definitely took some big blows in Year 12, and I ended up bottling it all up and going through some particularly dark episodes. But it's the little things about music and being surrounded by it that really get you through. It's the fact that a room feels empty without some tune playing, the fact that your foot automatically starts tapping whenever anything comes on, the fact that you'd voluntarily sit for hours on end in an orchestra and call it your happy place -- the fact that it lets you breathe. It's the little things like cool, unpredictable chords and delicious, interrupted cadences -- the things we do for a surprising vi chord.

At the end of the day, if you've got yourself into undertaking Music 2 or Music Extension, I doubt that you're going to let go of music the second you set down your pen after the written exam. Music has travelled with you a long way, and so it will continue to be your company. Perhaps you're going to pursue a career in music, or perhaps it'll become a favourite recreation. The wonderful thing about undertaking a Major Work is that you end up with something more tangible than a mark: a composition, the satisfaction of performance, an impressive ability. It's a subject that definitely relies a lot on independent study, practice, and growth It also requires you to work in concert (quite literally) with your peers and the musical community around you.

So get yourself acclimatised to that atonality, spell your composers' names correctly, and you'll *accel.* through the HSC in no time. Or maybe compound time.

PDHPE AND EARTH AND ENVIRONMENTAL SCIENCE

By Lucy Stevenson

Introduction

About Me

Hi! I'm Lucy Stevenson. I achieved an ATAR of 98.50 and was Dux of my High School, Northern Beaches Christian School, in 2018. I also achieved First in the New South Wales for PDHPE and Second in New South Wales for Earth and Environmental Science.

In February 2019, I will be commencing a Bachelor of Medical Sciences at Macquarie University and I intend to carry out further postgraduate study in the field of Medicine.

I believe that while high school can be academically challenging, it can be balanced out with enjoyable social time. Thus, throughout my HSC year, I ensured that I did not solely focus on my studies and I maintained solid support systems. I did this through effective time management.

Time Management

Time management skills are crucial to achieving academic success. I maintained a diary throughout the year, in which I wrote down the homework and readings that were required and assignments that were due. I also utilised a study planner, not only planning out when I would be studying throughout the week, but also making time for social events, paid work and personal time to relax as well.

Before each school term began, I wrote up a term plan for each subject, allocating specific weeks to specific syllabus dot points in order to keep organised and stay on top of the work load. This ensured that my study notes and flashcards were up to date, and that before each set of exams I already knew the content, so that I was refreshing my memory rather than learning content for the first time. This enabled me to spend more time writing practice essays, answering HSC style questions and applying my knowledge to sources.

During the school term I tended to study for 6 hours per day on the weekend (using 1.5 hours per day for homework and readings, 1.5 hours per day for writing study notes and flashcards, and 3 hours per day to work on assignments). On weekdays, I tended to study as soon as I got home, which was around 4 pm until 8 pm, using this time to consolidate what I had learnt in class by finishing study notes and ensuring that I had completed my set readings and homework. I also allocated 1 hour each afternoon to working on assignments.

In the school holidays, I tended to have the weekends off and study more intensively during the week. Throughout the HSC I found that I studied most optimally in the morning, so during the week I would study for 4 hours in the morning and 2 hours in the afternoon, leaving the rest of the day to relax and participate in social activities.

Example Term 2 Holiday Study Timetable Week 1

	Monday	Tuesday	Wednesday	Thursday	Friday
6:00-7:00 AM	Biology Past Paper (2010 HSC)	General Mathematics Past Paper	Biology Flashcards (Core 1)	General Mathematics Past Paper	Biology Practice Questions for Core 1 (Maintaining a Balance)
7:00-8:00 AM	Biology Past Paper (2010 HSC)	General Mathematics Past Paper	Biology Flashcards (Core 2)	General Mathematics Past Paper	Biology Practice Questions for Core 2 (Blueprint of Life)
8:00-9:00 AM	English Notes for Module B	EES Past Trial Paper (2015) - Only Core 1 and 2 Questions	Discovery Creative Piece Editing	EES Core 3 Past Questions booklet	Practice Essay for Discovery
9:00-10:00 AM	Work on Quote Table for Mod A	EES Core 1 Flashcards	Work on Quote Table for Mod B	EES Core 2 Flashcards	EES Core 3 Flashcards
10:00-11:00 AM	BREAK	BREAK	BREAK	BREAK	BREAK
11:00-12:00 PM	PDH/PE Flashcards (Core 1)	Modern History: WW1 Mindmaps	PDH/PE Flashcards (Core 2)	Modern History: Germany Essay Plans (2010, 2011 HSC)	2015 HSC PDH/PE Past Paper
12:00-1:00 PM	Health Priorities in Australia Practice Questions Booklet	Modern History: 2015 HSC Source Analysis Questions	Factors Affecting Performance Practice Questions Booklet	Modern History: 2016 HSC Source Analysis Questions	2015 HSC PDH/PE Past Paper

In the timetable above, there are a few aspects which are crucial to ensure success.

1. I never wrote down just the subject in a specific time slot. Instead, I always ensured that I wrote a **detailed plan** so that I could be as organised and efficient with my study time as possible. For example, in my Monday 6:00–8:00 am slot, instead of writing just

"Biology", I wrote down the specific past paper that I would be completing.

2. Always **take breaks**. I found that I could study for around 3 to 4 hours before I needed a break. I would usually use this time to do something productive, such as going for a walk or having something to eat.

3. I could only study during the morning or early afternoon. I found throughout my high school years that I was most alert during the morning and so I utilised this time to study. I think that all students should **consider when they study most optimally** before constructing a study plan, as this ensures that they are able to utilise their time most efficiently.

Motivation

Throughout the HSC I consistently heard my teachers saying, "The HSC is a marathon not a sprint", and this is crucial to keep in mind in order to prevent burning out. Before the HSC began, I came up with a goal ATAR and the marks I wished to achieve in each subject, as well as the degree which I was aiming to get into. This intrinsic motivation aided my success, as through each great mark I achieved I knew that I was chipping away at the ultimate goal, my ATAR.

Finding motivation can be difficult for some students, and to these students I would highly recommend spending 15 to 20 minutes writing down a goal for each subject you are sitting in the HSC.

Example

Earth and Environmental Science

Goal: To achieve a score of 90 in the HSC Trial Examinations.

How? Complete 2 past papers per week and seek feedback from my teacher. Get a friend/sibling to test me on my flashcards at least 4 times per week.

** It is important to note that while there is a clear goal, a time period is set and the action to be taken is also outlined clearly, so the goal can be achieved more easily.

In addition, for students who are struggling finding motivation to study, I would suggest setting a timer for 30 minutes of study, then doing something enjoyable, such as going for a run or reading a segment of a magazine.

Stress Management

During exam periods and when multiple assessments are due, students may feel overwhelmed and stressed. To manage stress I had three main ways:

1. Have a **solid study plan**. Know what you are doing each day and write down a set of goals for each study session. For Example:

Subject	Time Allocated	Syllabus	Points
PDH/PE	6:00am-7:30 AM	Factors Affecting Performance Question 1: How does training affect performance?	1. Energy Systems 2. Types of training and training methods 3. Principles of training 4. Physiological adaptations

2. **Write all your notes and flashcards BEFORE the exam period.** This way you can use your study time most effectively. Work out which areas of the syllabus you know and which you need to study in heavier detail by completing past paper questions.

3. Ensure you **balance your time,** and spend time with friends and exercise!

PDH/PE

PDH/PE is an extremely syllabus based subject, meaning that the questions in the HSC exam and HSC trials never venture very far past the syllabus itself. In essence, it makes this subject easy to prepare for when it comes to the exam period, and thus can provide students with rewarding results.

General Advice

1. Flashcards

I utilised flashcards for PDH/PE as it was an easy way to learn both the syllabus and the additional information. It's the additional information that differentiates the band 4 or 5 students from band 6. In addition, flashcards are an excellent way to test your knowledge before diving into past papers, so you become aware of the areas within the syllabus that you should focus more heavily on.

Chiropractic: Chiropractic is a form of alternative medicine mostly concerned with the diagnosis and treatment of mechanical disorders of the musculoskeletal system, especially the spine. Some proponents, especially those in the field's early history, have claimed that such disorders affect general health via the nervous system.
Aromatherapy: Aromatherapy uses plant materials and aromatic plant oils, including essential oils, and other aroma compounds for improving psychological or physical well-being.
Naturopathy: A system of alternative medicine based on the theory that diseases can be successfully treated or prevented without the use of drugs, by techniques such as control of diet, exercise and massage.
Acupuncture: Acupuncture is a form of alternative medicine in which thin needles are inserted into the body. It is a key component of traditional Chinese medicine (TCM). TEM theory and practice are not based upon scientific knowledge, and acupuncture is a pseudoscience.

> **Meditation:** Meditation can be defined as a practice where an individual focuses their mind on a particular object, thought or activity to achieve a mentally clear and emotionally calm state. Meditation may be used to reduce stress, anxiety, depression, and pain. It may be done while sitting, repeating a mantra, and closing the eyes in a quiet environment.
>
> **Massage:** The rubbing and kneading of muscles and joints of the body with the hands, especially to relieve tension or pain.
>
> **Homeopathy:** a system of complementary medicine in which ailments are treated by minute doses of natural substances that in larger amounts would produce symptoms of that ailment.

For this syllabus dot point I have the definition of each of the alternative health care therapies I was required to learn, as well as a statistic which may be used as evidence in a HSC response. On the opposite side of the card I have the syllabus dot point.

2. Past Papers

I am aware that every teacher tells their students to complete past papers, but it is not just the number of past papers you complete but how you utilise the papers. I had a highly supportive PDH/PE teacher who I actively sought feedback from after I completed each past paper; from this feedback I learnt how to structure my writing in a more effective way, so the HSC markers would be more inclined to give me marks. In addition, I utilised past papers to work on the areas of the syllabus that I struggled with the most.

3. Mind Maps

Another study technique I found useful was drawing out mind maps for more denser areas of the syllabus. I would draw out a mind map on an A3 piece of paper and write out all the content for the specific area of the syllabus along with the examples or statistics I could draw on in my response.

There are two main ways to use these mind maps. I would stick them up on the back of my door and on my wall so they would be there all the time for me to read them out loud. Secondly, I would use them as a supplementary study tool for the 'Read, Cover, Check, Write' technique.

4. 'Read, Cover, Check, Write'

The 'Read, Cover, Check, Write Technique' was especially helpful when I was learning statistics for the Health Priorities in Australia Unit. This technique allows you to consistently test your memory, and I found that when I wrote down my statistics they stuck in my head for longer periods of time. I often utilised this technique closer to the exam period, as it enabled me to remember specific details more quickly and enhanced my ability to memorise larger amounts of detailed information.

5. Going beyond the syllabus

As I touched upon previously, PDH/PE is a highly syllabus based subject; however, what differentiated top students in the cohort from average students is the ability to add detail into their responses and to go beyond the syllabus dot point. This can be achieved in several ways. For example, you can use statistics or research from a credible source, such as a government epidemiological study, or a Non-Government Organisation webpage, such as the Cancer Council. These sources provide up to date statistics and information. The additional details which you can add into your response enhance the point you are trying to make in your response, which essentially shows the marker that you have an in-depth knowledge of the subject or syllabus point, .

One of the best resources you can access to source statistics for the Health Priorities in Australia core is "Australia's Health 2018".

https://www.aihw.gov.au/reports/australias-health/australias-health-2018/contents/table-of-contents

Exam Tips

1. Use the PEEL Structure

When answering a HSC Question, the PEEL structure is one of the best ways to offer a thorough response. I used this format throughout Year 11 and 12, and I found that it enabled me to respond to the question most effectively. The PEEL Structure is as follows:

P: Point

Present a micro-introduction which allows you to directly answer the question being asked. This is usually one to two sentences long.

E: Example/Evidence

By giving a clear example of what you are talking about, this part of your paragraph allows you to show the marker your in-depth knowledge of the subject area . For example, if you were to write an example of a measure of epidemiology, such as infant mortality rate, it would convey to the marker that you have a more in-depth knowledge of the syllabus.

E: Expand

In this section of the paragraph, you further explain the meaning and significance of the example you have given previously. This section allows you to add more depth to your response.

L: Link

The last section of your paragraph should allow you to make a close connection between the knowledge you have shared with the marker to the question you are responding to.

2. Cite Examples

It is crucial to include a number of examples within your answer in order to gain maximum marks and write a well rounded response. By giving examples you are showcasing extensive knowledge of the syllabus area.

3. Take your time and plan ahead

While completing a HSC exam it can be easy to get caught up with insufficient remaining time to answer all the question.. Before each exam I tended to create a "plan of attack", in which I would plan out how much time to spend for each section and in which order I would complete the sections.

For example: HSC PDH/PE Exam, 3 hours (9:05am-12:05pm)

Firstly, I would complete the short answer questions; I found these questions most manageable and the statistics for the examples easiest to remember. Then I would complete the options section of the paper, as this would require the most time and the longest responses. I would do this in the middle of the exam, as this is when I was most focused and 'in the zone'. Finally, I would complete the multiple choice, as this would be easier to complete if I had struggled on previous questions and was running out of time.

An Example HSC Style Question

When answering a HSC style question, it is important to start by underlining or highlighting the verb at the beginning on the question. In this case, it is "compare". If you are asked to "compare", it means you must show how things are similar or different.

Compare institutional and non-institutional health facilities and services. (3 Marks)

> *An institutional health facility is one that is run by government or private organisations, providing healthcare in a structured format. For example, psychiatric hospitals and pubic hospitals are institutional health care services as patients may utilise these facilities over a longer period of time. On the other hand, non-institutional health care facilities are less structured facilities in*

which individuals can seek out. These facilities in essence are where patients seek treatment then leave immediately. There are a number of experts within the Australian health system which provide this type of care, including Psychiatrists and General Practitioners. Thus, institutional health care facilities are services are those which are performed in a structured setting while non-institutional health services and facilities are those which are performed in less structured manner and over a lesser period of time.

Notes and Organisation

1. Importance of the syllabus

As mentioned previously, PDH/PE is structured in a manner which makes the subject easy to study, for as it distinctively syllabus based. My notes for PDH/PE were structured in a way that included the syllabus dot point as the heading and further breakdown of the syllabus in sub headings. This way I made sure my notes were easy to read. Here's an example of my "Stages of Skill Acquisition" notes.

How does the acquisition of skill affect performance?

Stages of skill acquisition:

Cognitive: The cognitive stage should focus on fundamental skills, aim to keep motivation high and provide positive, constructive and specific feedback. The fundamental requirement in the cognitive stage is understanding the nature of skill. Individuals focus on the task required by watching, thinking, reasoning and visualizing the skill rather than practicing it. Demonstrations are critical during this stage, demonstrations should be accompanied with simple instructions to avoid information overload. Complex skills may need to be broke down into smaller movements. It is expected that the learner may experience some errors; poor timing, disorientation.

E.g. When playing a golf shot, a learner in the cognitive stage will often miss the ball or hit the ground.

Associative: The associative stage is characterized by an emphasis on practice. The learner, having acquired an idea of what the skill consists of, needs to repeat the movements to develop the synchronization of their mind and muscles. The focus should be on temporal patterning. The player should be familiar with subroutines and work on assembling them into the required skill. Errors are still prominent in this stage, but are smaller and less frequent than in the cognitive stage. Feedback is again essential. A sense of fluency and refinement of skill develops as the learner's kinesthetic sense improves. Gradually, the confidence of the learner increases. For complex skills, some learners remain in the stage for long period of time.

(Stages of skill acquisition notes sample.)

In this set of my syllabus notes I used a bold font to show the key words which relate to the syllabus dot point. I also used examples and expanded upon these examples, so when I completed a past paper my writing would be clear and concise.

Earth And Environmental Science

Earth and Environmental Science is a highly technical subject which requires an in-depth knowledge of all aspects of the syllabus. To achieve high results in this subject, I believe that visual learning is the best way to understand the specifics of complex scientific processes.

General Advice

1. Mind Maps

Mind maps are the best way to display information relating to the syllabus, as there are a lot of specific pieces of information, processes and diagrams which are easier to display in this format. I generally wrote the syllabus dot point in the middle of the page and added the related information as well as diagrams which are related to this topic. As I am a visual learner, this process aided my study; through the visualisation of images and colours I could remember geological processes more accurately.

2. Past Papers

Once again past papers are a useful tool to decipher which areas of the syllabus you are struggling with. They are also a good opportunity to practice writing in the formal style which best suits a HSC science unit and using vocabulary which is relevant to the specific syllabus area. I mostly used Earth and Environmental Science past papers to remember my examples and to draw diagrams for the different geological processes that had to be memorised.

3. Drawings and Diagrams

Drawings and diagrams are important to Earth and Environmental Science as they are frequently referenced within the HSC exam. During my HSC studies, I had diagrams of all the major geological processes as well as the rocks associated with these processes. I put these diagrams on my wall so I would see them regularly and learning the syllabus information even when I wasn't "studying".

In addition, within the HSC exams and HSC trials, students are often required to answer a question by drawing a diagram. Therefore, by practising these diagrams it becomes easier to achieve optimal marks.

4. Colour Coding Your Syllabus

In order to study most effectively, I found that colour coding my syllabus was the best way to identify the areas of the syllabus that I found most challenging. I used a system whereby each of three colours (Red, Yellow and Green) represented my level of knowledge:

Green: The area of the syllabus I knew well and had detailed quotes/examples for.
Yellow: The area of the syllabus I still had patchy knowledge of.
Red: The area of the syllabus which I had little to no knowledge of.

	Students learn to:	Students:
1 Evidence from early Earth indicates the first life forms survived in changing habitats during the Archean and Proterozoic eons	• identify that geological time is divided into eons on the basis of fossil evidence of different life forms • define cyanobacteria as simple photosynthetic organisms and examine the fossil evidence of cyanobacteria in Australia • outline the processes and environmental conditions involved in the deposition of a Banded Iron Formation (BIF) • examine and explain processes involved in fossil formation and the range of fossil types • outline stable isotope evidence for the first presence of life in 3.8×10^9 year-old rocks	• gather and process information from secondary sources to draw up a timeline to compare the relative lengths of the Hadean, Archaean, Proterozoic and Phanerozoic eons • gather and analyse information from secondary sources to explain the significance of the Banded Iron Formations as evidence of life in primitive oceans • gather, analyse and present information from secondary sources on the habitat of modern stromatolites and use available evidence to propose possible reasons for their reduced abundance and distribution in comparison with ancient stromatolites

(Example of colour coded Earth and Environmental Science Syllabus)

Exam Tips

1. Read the full question.

Some of the HSC style questions for EES can trick students as they may be highly specific and requite in-depth knowledge of specific aspects of the syllabus. To ensure you get the best marks possible, I believe that analysing what the question is actually asking is a key step. I did this through a two-step process:

Step 1: Highlighting the key words of the question.

By highlighting the key words you are able to understand the specifics of the question: which verb is being used and how much depth the question is asking you to go into. Therefore, by taking a small amount of time to go through the question, you are giving yourself extra marks, as you are ensuring that you are giving an answer your marker is looking for.

Step 2: Taking 30 seconds to jot down an example.

Do this when you are analyzing the question. Having examples is important to showcasing extensive knowledge to the marker. Without having specific examples you are not showing that you know how to apply your answer to scientific or geological processes. When I studied for Earth and Environmental Science I ensured that I always had at least one example for the different plate boundaries, rock types, volcanoes or even earthquakes. In this case, I could apply not only the knowledge from my textbook but showcase further in-depth knowledge by presenting extra examples.

2. Fully label your diagrams.

In an exam it is important that you fully label the diagram with as much detail as possible if you get a question which requires a diagram. When studying for my exams throughout Year 12, I had labelled diagrams on my walls showing specific plate boundaries, volcano types and associated rock types. These clearly labelled examples were useful tools for testing my memory, which enhanced my ability to recall these diagrams in an exam scenario.

3. Meticulously check your tables and charts.

Tables and charts are easy marks to access in an exam, but unfortunately they are also where students tend to make the most mistakes, thus losing easy marks. To ensure you get optimal marks in this section of the exam, use the checklist I always followed in my mind:

1. Labels/Titles

2. Pencil

3. Averages (if applicable)

4. Line of best fit

5. Units of measurement

6. X and Y axis (It is important to remember that the dependent variable goes on the "Y" Axis and the independent variable goes on the "X" Axis.)

Final Advice

Good Luck in your HSC studies! Always ensure that you have a good work-study balance. The hard work you put in now is something that you will never regret at the conclusion of your HSC studies.

AFTERWORD

After reading this book, hopefully you have discovered a few tips and tricks to unlock your true potential. The people who have contributed to this volume have all performed their highest achievements, and it's our hope that, in the very near future, you will be able to do so as well.

However, this promise of success comes with one very big caveat: your willingness to work hard. It has been mentioned before, but let it be said again, that in the HSC "hard work beats talent when talent doesn't work hard." It's up to you to take these tips and apply them to your own study, your own circumstance, and your own exams. It's up to you to constantly refresh your notes, increase your knowledge and practice those past papers.

This is your race, and no one else can run it for you.

On the flipside though, don't see this as pressure. You get out of the HSC what you want to get out of it, so don't feel as if you had to push yourself harder than you want to. There's no point punishing yourself to get somewhere you don't even want to go. Take the time to zoom out, to question what you're doing, why you're doing it, and put it all in perspective.

Indeed, graduating is a very weird feeling. For about six months, it is last after last after last. As the big day countdown on your Mac wallpaper ticks down, you have graduation, valedictory, formal, your first, third and then last HSC exam. Then it's over.

Your whole world has built up to this one, huge moment, the end of it all. You put so much pressure on yourself to perform, you feel so much anxiety and stress and excitement for it all to be over. And, then, just like that, it is.

Yet these emotions don't release in a flood of cathartic joy happiness, and ecstasy in freedom. Instead, they merely dissipate meekly into the ether. You ask yourself, where to next?

You're in limbo, waiting for something to happen to you, for you.

It's like in Tim Winton's short story, "Big World", where Biggy and our (intentionally) nameless narrator drive down the highway, to nowhere in particular, searching for something to do with their lives. There's the excitement of the trip, the trepidation of the unknown and the joy of pushing beyond the bleak boundaries of the town they call home. As their car breaks down on the Nullaboor, Winton provides a perfect image of tranquillity and quiet, where everything seems "impossibly far off". As their bomb of a car spits acidic fumes, the narrator looks forward to the far-off distant future, to his own family, the re-evaluation of his life goals and the loss of his best mate. Yet, in that transient, ephemeral moment, as the dying sun collapses behind the cracked horizon, it is all unimaginable. Winton writes, the world gets "suddenly so big around us, so big we just give in and watch."

As Winton implores us to do, take that time. Take that time to sit back, relax, and watch it all unfold. You have the opportunity to build something truly special during Year 12. Indeed, it is the formative year that really kick starts the rest of your life. So, enjoy it! Don't take it too seriously and have fun, because there isn't much point doing much else.

Finally, good luck with it all from the Catch Up with Top Achievers team. We sincerely hope that you got something out of this book, achieve the results that you want, get to where you want to go, and, above all, enjoy doing it.

ACKNOWLEDGEMENTS

As I handed in my final HSC exam paper, strangely, I did not feel relieved, but I became more anxious. What happens now? People often told me that the HSC isn't the end, but they've never mentioned what will come afterwards. Since an early age, I've always wanted to create things. I've always wanted to become an inventor.

In the making of this book, I've realised that simply having ideas is far from enough. Ideas are flimsy, unless they are brought to fruition. None of what you read in this book would have been possible without my friends, family and colleagues.

As I conclude editing this book, I'm overwhelmed with gratitude.

Firstly, I would like to thank the contributors of this book. More specifically (last name in alphabetic order), John Bivell, Alexandra Christopoulos, Drew Ireland-Shead, Lucinda Krek, Eleanor Lawton-Wade, Lucy Stevenson, Belinda Thomas, Jenny Wang, Jesse Wright, Tim Yang and Zoe Zhang. You guys are the cornerstones of this project; this book would not have been possible without you. Your wise words will inspire many more future Top-Achievers.

To Helena Budiarto, my English teacher at Cranbrook:

You were like a second mum to me throughout my senior years. Not only that you made the learning of English fun again, you also taught me many life lessons that I will cherish forever. I will always remember the chicken congee you made for us on Monday mornings to calm down our nerves before the exams. When I first brought my ideas to you, unlike many other people, you saw the potential of my book and you were kind enough to read through the proposal and give me many useful feedback.

To my editing team, Fionn Parker and James Drielsma:

I am forever grateful for knowing that you guys will have my back. Working with you two not only simplified the entire process, but also allowed me to become more mature as a person.

To Felix Lee, a great business mind, who refreshed my naivety when it comes to doing business. I can vividly remember the lecture you gave me when I first started this project. It has helped me tremendously throughout the process.

To Tao Zhao, senior publisher/editor:

Your succinct wise words on book publishing surpassed everything I have read. You opened my mind about many future possibilities for this project, many of which I have planned to explore.

To Yuqing Zhang, Editor-in-Chief of China Radio International:

You were kind enough to take out an hour of your valuable time to educate me about the industry of book publishing at the very beginning of this project. Your words definitely gave me a clear direction and reduced many unnecessary detours.

To Huaiyu Wang, my editor and Grzegorz Japoł, my graphic designer:

Thank you for doing your job so perfectively and efficiently, making the entire process much quicker.

To Ryan Sadler, the Head of Mathematics at Cranbrook:

I looked forward to attending your class the most every single day because you are always charged with positivity. You have taught me so much more than just mathematics.

To Joseph Guss, my physics teacher at Cranbrook:

Words cannot express my gratitude to your teaching. Before I met you, I'd always thought that learning is restricted in the classroom, but after learning from you, I realised the importance of having a curious mind that wants to explore more. From playing the guitar to explain how waves oscillate, to telling us stories about many unrelated science topics, I'm grateful for having a teacher like you.

To Angelique Sanders, my House Master at Cranbrook:

You provided me with many valuable opportunities throughout high school. I'll be forever grateful for your guidance.

To all the teachers who have enlightened me throughout my time at Cranbrook. I thank you all. Attending Cranbrook has been the best decision so far in my life. I learnt so much more than what is in the book.

To Richard Li, my mathematics tutor from Richard Coaching:

Your simple sayings have been guiding me to where I wanted to be. "Make it happen." It's so simple, yet so profound.

To Yuhao Chen, one of my best friends:

The initial street survey we did together was definitely the most memorable. Having you to push me to approach strangers helped me to become more confident. Our efforts have finally paid off. Ovuvuevuevue Enyetuenwuevue Ugbemugbem Osas!

To Yuan Zhou, my best friend:

Words will not be able to express my gratitude to you. Your daily vulgarities have become more vulgar as we age. I don't know where I would be today without your constant support and those vulgarities. You are a brother to me.

To Lin Xu-Zhang, a great artist:

Thank you for your consistent support and consultation throughout the process. Your determination through adversity is truly inspiring. I look forward to seeing you on the big stage one day.

Finally, I would like to show my appreciations towards my parents, who have been supporting me since the very beginning. The idea of this book actually came from my Dad, Zhiping, who wrote a similar book before when he first graduated from high school.

To Dad:

You provided me with many essential resources that have helped me throughout this process. Your stories inspire and motivate me to do greater things.

To Mum:

You pushed me to where I am today. When I thought about quitting, you always had my back and pushed me to accomplish a little bit more each time. I wish time could go slower.

As always, the best things are yet to come.

April 2019

By Adam Ma

www.ingramcontent.com/pod-product-compliance
Lightning Source LLC
Chambersburg PA
CBHW032037290426
44110CB00012B/845